Upper–Intermediate

Workbook with key

New Headway

English Course

Liz & John Soars
with Jo Devoy

Oxford University Press

Contents

The tense system
Auxiliary verbs
have/have got

The tense system

1 Identifying tenses

1 Write in the correct verb form, using the verb in **bold**.

walk

a Our baby Jack _____ now. He's just twelve months old.

b 'How did you get here?'
'We _____ . It didn't take long.'

c After ten miles I had to stop for a rest. We _____ non-stop for four hours.

take

d My dog looked guilty. He _____ some food from the kitchen table.

e It was a hard match. At half-time, one of the footballers _____ to hospital.

f 'This shirt is £45, sir.'
'That's fine. I _____ it.'

have

g I think we should buy a new car.
We _____ this one for ages.

h Don't phone at 8.00 this evening.
We _____ dinner then.

i We _____ a lovely picnic until my wife was stung by a bee.

make

j This is a great sandwich shop. Everything _____ freshly _____ .

k By the time I'm forty I _____ enough money to retire.

l Have you heard about Lenny?
He _____ redundant.

wash

m 'Where are my jeans?' 'They _____ at the moment. Sorry.'

n My favourite white T-shirt went pink.
It _____ with my daughter's red sweater.

o 'Why are you all wet?' 'I _____ the car.'

sell

p I wish I'd bought that antique chair I saw in the shop window. It _____ by now.

q My sister earns a good salary. She _____ life insurance policies.

r If no one offers to buy the house, it _____ by auction next month.

teach

s At the end of this term I _____ for six years.

t The soldiers _____ how to use grenades when unfortunately one blew up and injured them.

2 Complete the tense chart with the verb forms from Exercise 1. There is one for each gap.

Active	Simple	Continuous
Present		
Past		
Future		
Present Perfect		
Past Perfect		
Future Perfect		
Passive	Simple	Continuous
Present		
Past		
Future		
Present Perfect		
Past Perfect		
Future Perfect		

2 Correcting mistakes

Three of the sentences in this exercise are correct. Put a tick (✔) next to them. All the other sentences contain mistakes. Put a cross (✗) next to them and correct them.

Example

✗ I ~~work~~ hard at the moment because I have exams next week.
I'm working

a ☐ It's been really cold lately, so I've bought some new thermal underwear.

_____

b ☐ Manchester United play really well at the moment. Their new player has real talent.

_____

c ☐ I've heard you'll have a baby! Congratulations.

_____

d ☐ Was Tim working in Barcelona while you were working in Madrid?

_____

e ☐ When I was a little girl, I've always spent my pocket money on sweets.

_____

f ☐ I went out with Paul for two years now, and we're still crazy about each other.

_____

g ☐ I can't decide what to buy my brother for his birthday. Perhaps I'm going to get him a new shirt.

_____

h ☐ She'd trained so hard for the Olympics that I felt sure she would get at least a bronze medal.

_____

i ☐ A one-day strike has called by London Underground staff for Friday this week.

_____

j ☐ The teacher said that Megan had been working hard and was deserved to pass all her exams.

_____

3 Choosing the right tense

T 1.1 Read the telephone conversation between Mr Lewis and June, the travel agent. Put the verbs into the correct tense. Sometimes there is more than one possibility.

A holiday in South Africa

J Good morning. Fairweather Travel, June speaking. How can I help you?

Mr L Good morning. I (**a**) _____ (look) at your brochure on holidays in Cape Town and the Western Cape and I (**b**) _____ (wonder) if you could give me some more information?

J Certainly. Mr …?

Mr L It's Lewis, Mr Lewis.

J Well, as it happens, Mr Lewis, I (**c**) _____ (go) to Cape Town myself last Christmas. I (**d**) _____ never _____ (be) there before. I (**e**) _____ (do) some research for Fairweather Travel, so I (**f**) _____ (get) to know the city pretty well.

Mr L Really! Then you're just the person to talk to. Tell me, (**g**) _____ you _____ (feel) safe? There (**h**) _____ (be) so much unrest in South Africa recently.

J Well, Mr Lewis, I (**i**) _____ (visit) many countries on behalf of Fairweather Travel, and I have to say that I (**j**) _____ (feel) very safe the whole time I (**k**) _____ (travel) round South Africa.

Mr L That's reassuring. My three children (**l**) _____ (learn) all about South Africa at school. They (**m**) _____ (look forward) to seeing Table Mountain. My wife (**n**) _____ (hope) to sample some South African wine. (**o**) _____ that _____ (be) possible?

J Oh, yes indeed. There are tours to many of the vineyards and wine cellars. Your wife (**p**) _____ (be able) to try some really good wines. South Africa (**q**) _____ (produce) some of the best wine and brandy in the world.

Mr L How interesting. Well, you (**r**) _____ (be) most helpful. I (**s**) _____ (get) back to you as soon as possible, after I (**t**) _____ (discuss) it all with my wife. Thank you very much. Goodbye.

J Goodbye.

Passives

4 Active or passive?

1 These sentences sound unnatural in the active. Rewrite them using the passive.

a They don't make Volvos in Norway.

Volvos _____

b They built our house in the 17th century.

Our house _____

c Has someone decorated your bedroom?

_____

d Someone's decorating my bedroom at the moment.

My bedroom _____

e We moved out of our house while they were building the extension.

While the extension _____

_____

f We arrived home from holiday to find someone had burgled our house.

_____

_____

g They won't recognize her in those dark glasses.

She _____

2 Put the verbs in brackets into the correct tense, active or passive.

a The robbers _____ (catch) as they _____ (leave) the bank.

b Jo _____ (arrive) home to find feathers everywhere. Her cat _____ (catch) a bird.

c Our dustbins _____ (empty) on a Monday.

d Mr Taylor was furious with the newsagent because his Sunday newspaper _____ (not deliver).

e It's a very upsetting time for Aunt Mary. Her budgie _____ (miss) for three days now.

f Why _____ you _____ (not like) going to the opera? We _____ (love) it. We _____ (see) *La Bohème* next Saturday.

g We _____ (drive) down a quiet country lane when suddenly we _____ (overtake) by a police car.

h When I woke up this morning, the world looked like a wonderland. It _____ (snow) all night.

i Don't worry. When you _____ (arrive) in New York, you _____ (pick up) by one of our drivers and taken to the conference centre.

5 At home on a train

1 Read about Pat and Ronald Thomas, who live on a train. Put the verb in brackets into the correct verb form, active or passive.

At home on a train

Pat and Ronald Thomas (a) _____ (not live) in a caravan, but their home **(b)** _____ (travel) more miles than any other house in Britain! Their house **(c)** _____ (make) from a pair of Victorian railway carriages, and they **(d)** _____ (live) there for ten years. 'I **(e)** _____ (not want) to live in a train at first,' admits Pat, 'but when I **(f)** _____ (see) that this train had a garden with a stream, I just **(g)** _____ (fall) in love with it. We **(h)** _____ (buy) it from an old lady, and she **(i)** _____ already _____ (do) a lot of work on it. But there is a lot left to do and we **(j)** _____ still _____ (make) improvements.'

Visitors are often surprised to see how spacious the house is. All the dividing walls **(k)** _____ (remove), so now the rooms are about fifteen metres long.

Pat and Ronald **(l)** _____ (pay) £68,000 for their house. Recently they **(m)** _____ (offer) more than £100,000 for it, but it's not for sale.

'I **(n)** _____ (discover) more and more about the history of this train all the time,' says Ronald. 'It **(o)** _____ (build) in Swindon between 1855 and 1875. We **(p)** _____ (work) so hard to make it beautiful that I don't think we **(q)** _____ ever _____ (sell) it,' he admits. 'I hope it **(r)** _____ (remain) in our family forever.'

2 Here are the answers to some questions about Pat and Ronald. Write the questions.

a _____ *in a caravan*?

No, they don't. They live in a pair of railway carriages.

b _____?

For ten years.

c _____ *from*?

An old lady.

d _____?

£68,000.

e _____

_____?

More than £100,000.

f _____?

In Swindon between 1855 and 1875.

g _____?

Yes, they are. They want to make it even more beautiful.

h _____?

No, they won't. They want it to remain in the family forever.

Auxiliary verbs

6 *have*, *be*, or *do*?

Put the correct form of *have*, *be*, or *do* in the gap. Write **A** or **F** next to each sentence to show whether it is used as an **auxiliary** verb or a **full** verb. Sometimes the auxiliary is negative.

Example

[A] They *had* finished supper when we arrived.

[F] We *had* pizza for supper last night.

a ☐ It _____ been a lovely day. Thank you.

b ☐ I _____ my homework very quickly yesterday evening.

c ☐ I always _____ a shower after work.

d ☐ I _____ always had a passion for Indian food.

e ☐ Jane _____ not at work today because

☐ she _____ a bad back.

f ☐ Graham overslept, so he _____ catch his train.

g ☐ What have you _____ to your hair? You look awful!

h ☐ What _____ your new boyfriend look like?

i ☐ This self-portrait _____ painted by Van Gogh.

j ☐ My car _____ repaired at the moment.

k ☐ I hate _____ the washing-up. I'd like

☐ _____ a dishwasher.

l ☐ I've _____ doing this exercise for ages and

☐ I _____ fed up!

have and have got

⚠

1 *Have* and *have got* are both used to express present possession.

Do you **have** │ any brothers or sisters?
Have you **got** │

Yes, │ I **do**. I **have** │ two brothers.
│ I **have**. I**'ve got** │

2 *Have to* can be replaced with *have got to* for present obligation.

Do you **have to** │ go now?
Have you **got to** │

Yes, │ I **do**. I **have to** │ catch the bus.
│ I **have**. I**'ve got to** │

3 Only forms of *have* (not *have got*) are used in all other tenses.

I **had** my first car when I was nineteen.
I**'ve had** this car for two years.
I**'ll have** a strawberry ice-cream, please.
I**'d had** three cars by the time I was twenty.
I'd like **to have** a dog.
He loves **having** a sports car.

4 *Have* (not *have got*) is used in many expressions.

have breakfast   have a bath
have a party   have a good time
have fun   have a word with someone

5 *Have got* is generally more informal. It is used more in spoken English than in written English. However, they are often interchangeable.

Have with the *do/does* forms is more common in American English.

7 Forms of *have* and *have got*

1 **T 1.2** Complete the dialogues with a correct form of *have* or *have got*. Sometimes both forms are possible.

Example
You *had* a very noisy party last night.
How many friends *have* you *got*?

a 'Rebecca, _____ you _____ a headache?
You don't look very well.'

'No, it's not that. I _____ a baby and I feel sick.'

'Congratulations! Do you want a boy or a girl?'

'Well, I _____ three boys, so it would be nice

_____ a girl this time.'

b 'Jane, _____ you _____ any chocolate?'

'No, of course I _____ . I'm on a diet.'

'You're joking. You _____ two Mars Bars
yesterday.'

'I know, I _____ any willpower, but I really want
to be slim for my holiday next month.'

'Good luck!'

c 'Nick, I thought you _____ a company car.
Why are you cycling to work?'

'I _____ an accident last week. I drove through
a red light and hit a police car.'

'That's bad luck. _____ you _____ go to
court?'

'Yes, I will.'

d '_____ you _____ any pets?'

'No, we _____ . _____ you?'

'Oh yes. I _____ a dog all my life. At the moment

I _____ a dog, two cats, and two budgies.'

'I'd love _____ a dog, but I'm not so sure about
cats and budgies!'

e 'Come on! We _____ hurry. We're late!'

'But I _____ my passport. I can't find it
anywhere!'

'What! You _____ it yesterday. _____ a look
in your bag.'

'Thank goodness. It's here!'

f I'm looking forward to _____ a few days'

holiday. I _____ so much work for the past

couple of months, I _____ a break for ages.

2 Make the sentences negative.

a She's got blue eyes.

_____

b I usually have breakfast at 8.00.

_____

c I have a lot of money.

_____

d They're having a row about money.

_____

e We had a good time on holiday.

_____

f I have to work ten hours a day.

_____

g I had to get up at 6.00 this morning.

_____

3 Ask questions about the sentences in Exercise 2.

a What colour _____?
b What time _____?
c How much _____?
d What _____?
e _____ a good time on holiday?
f How many _____?
g What time _____?

Vocabulary

8 Rooms and their contents

Put the following objects in the right room.
Some objects can go into more than one room.

bidet	armchair	taps	dressing table
sink	high chair	cot	shower curtain
sofa	wardrobe	duvet	chest of drawers
pillow	washbasin	flannel	drinks cabinet
scales	bread bin	sheets	magazine rack
tin opener	ornaments	rug	Welsh dresser
tea towel	cat flap	quilt	French windows
towel rail	dishwasher	towel	

Kitchen	Living room	Bedroom	Bathroom

9 *house* and *home* idioms

1 Underline the correct definition for each idiom.
Use your dictionary.

a *That boy's eating us out of house and home.*
He's got a huge appetite.
He never eats at home.

b *They get on like a house on fire.*
They have a very good relationship.
They are always having arguments.

c *I could shop until the cows come home.*

I could shop
until dinner time.

I could shop for
a very long time.

d *These drinks are on the house.*
The drinks are home-made.
The drinks are free.

e *Andrew Lloyd Webber's new musical brought
the house down.*
The musical was a success.
The musical wasn't a success.

f *The television pictures really brought home to me
the horrors of the famine.*
The pictures made me realize fully the horrors of
the famine.
The pictures clearly showed the horrors of famine.

g *My mum brings home the bacon in our family.*
Mum buys the meat in our family.
Mum earns the money in our family.

h *Having won 57% of the votes in the election, Haig
was finally home and dry.*
Haig managed to win, although it wasn't easy.
Haig won the election without any difficulty.

2 **T 1.3** Complete the conversations with one of the
idioms above in the correct form.

a **A** I was so sorry to hear about your cat, Fluffy, dying.
B Thank you. When I saw her empty cat basket it
really _____ the fact that
I'd never see her again.

b **A** How was it when you met Andy's parents for the
first time?
B It was great. We all _____ .

c **A** You spend a fortune on food!
B Well, we've got two hungry teenagers. They

_____ .

d **A** Did you read those excellent reviews in the local
paper about the school play?
B Yes, I did. Apparently, it _____

e **A** You're always going to discos, Jenny. Don't you
ever get tired of them?
B No, never. I could dance _____

Phrasal verbs

10 Literal and idiomatic meanings

⚠️

Phrasal verbs sometimes have a literal meaning, and sometimes an idiomatic meaning.

I *looked up* the tree,
but I couldn't see my cat.
(Literal)

I *looked up* the spelling
in my dictionary.
(Idiomatic)

1 In this exercise the phrasal verbs are all used literally. Fill the gaps with a particle from the box. Some are used more than once.

away	on	off	back	out	down	in

a The dentist said my tooth was rotten. He had to pull it _____ .

b Don't run _____! Come here! I want to talk to you.

c My aunt fell _____ the stairs and broke her leg.

d And I fell _____ my horse!

e When the sun went _____ it was really cold.

f A button has come _____ my shirt. Could you sew it back _____ for me?

g I don't feel like cooking tonight. Shall we eat _____?

h I'm going to the library to take _____ the books I've finished.

i The washing is hanging up outside, and it's just started to rain. Can you help me to bring it _____?

j Don't throw that empty box _____ . I'm sure I can use it for something.

2 Fill the pairs of gaps with the same phrasal verb from the box. Put the phrasal verb in the correct form. Write **L** if its meaning is literal and **I** if it is idiomatic.

take off	fall out	pick up	sort out
put up	stand up	hold on	

a ☐ After my operation, all my hair _____ . It's growing back now, though.

  ☐ Jane and John _____ again last night. I could hear them arguing.

b ☐ I don't know how you _____ with your boyfriend. He's so unreliable.

  ☐ _____ your hand if you know the answer.

c ☐ I _____ all my clothes drawers today, so now I know where everything is.

  ☐ You and I have a problem of communication, but if we try hard I'm sure we can _____ it _____ .

d ☐ When I was at school, we had to _____ when the teacher came in the room.

  ☐ You shouldn't let your sister boss you about and tell you what to do all the time. You should _____ for yourself, and tell her what *you* want to do.

e ☐ (On the phone) 'Can I speak to Kate, please?' '_____ . I'll just get her.'

  ☐ When you're riding as a passenger on a motorbike, you have to _____ tight.

f ☐ It's too warm to be wearing a woolly jumper. Why don't you _____ it _____?

  ☐ My business really started to _____ after it was featured in the local newspapers.

g ☐ I was never taught how to cook. I just _____ it _____ from my mother.

  ☐ The baby's crying. Can you _____ him _____?

Pronunciation

11 Vowel sounds and spelling

> ⚠️ **Phonetic symbols** /fənetɪk sɪmbəlz/
>
> There is a list of phonetic symbols on the inside back cover of this Workbook.

1 **T 1.4** Look at the words in phonetics. Each of them contains a different English vowel sound. Read them aloud to yourself, then write the word next to the transcription. (They are all from Unit 1 of the Student's Book.)

a /frend/ _____

b /ɪŋglɪʃ/ _____

c /tʃiːz/ _____

d /mʌnθ/ _____

e /tʊk/ _____

f /hjuːdʒ/ _____

g /kræʃ/ _____

h /ʃɒk/ _____

i /θɔːt/ _____

j /ʃɜːt/ _____

k /tʃɑːt/ _____

l /tempə/ _____

2 **T 1.5** The chart shows the main English vowel sounds.

/e/	/ɪ/	/iː/	/ʌ/
letter	sick		

/ʊ/	/uː/	/æ/	/ɒ/

/ɔː/	/ɜː/	/ɑː/	/ə/

Write the words in the right box.
There are **four** words for each vowel sound.

~~sick~~	~~letter~~	good	cool	tree	suit	f**a**n
early	horse	w**ea**ther	log	c**a**mp	head	s**au**sage
hug	p**a**rty	lett**er**	w**o**men	jeans	fath**er**	floor
w**o**man	b**u**sy	could	work	walk	can**oe**	search
heat	mach**i**ne	m**o**ther	d**au**ghter	fun	garden	b**ui**lding
w**o**rry	odd	br**ea**kfast	p**u**llover	roof	want	m**a**chine
f**a**mily	f**a**ther	**a**ccent	ban**a**na	ban**a**na	worm	

3 Read these sentences aloud and then transcribe them.

a /lɜːnɪŋ ə fɒrən læŋgwɪdʒ ɪz veri juːsfʊl/

_____

b /ɪts ɪmpɔːtənt tə hæv ə gʊd dɪkʃənəri/

_____

c /ɪŋglɪʃ spelɪŋ ɪznt iːzi/

_____

d /ɪts gʊd tə kiːp lɪsts əv vəkæbjələri/

_____

e /græmə dʌznt hæv tə bi bɔːrɪŋ/

_____

f /evrɪwʌn wɒnts tə spiːk ɪŋglɪʃ fluːəntli/

_____

2 Present Perfect
Continuous verb forms
have something *done*

Present Perfect

1 Present Perfect simple or continuous?

1 Which sentence matches better in **A** and **B**?

	A	B
a	I've written I've been writing	to Auntie Fay to wish her happy birthday. my essay all morning.
b	I've lost I've been losing	weight recently. my car keys.
c	They've missed They've been missing	you lots, so come home soon. the train.
d	She's been talking She's talked	on the phone for ages. about this subject before.
e	Paula's been leaving Paula's left	work early today to meet her uncle. work late all this week.
f	The cat's been going The cat's gone	next door to have its dinner. upstairs.
g	He's had He's been having	a heart attack. second thoughts about accepting the job.
h	I've been saving up I've saved up	to buy a new stereo. about £200.
i	I've been swimming I've swum	twenty lengths today. which is why my hair is wet.
j	I've been finding I've found	my cheque book at last. it difficult to concentrate recently.

2 Put the verb in brackets into the Present Perfect simple or continuous.

> Example
> I *'ve been playing* (play) tennis all morning and I'm exhausted.

a Please drive carefully to work. It _____ (snow) and the roads are very slippery.

b How far _____ you _____ (travel) this morning?

c Kate and Paul _____ (live) in London for the past five years. Recently they _____ (try) to buy a house in the suburbs, but they _____ (not manage) to sell their flat yet.

d Jill and Andy _____ (argue) a lot recently, because Jill's always going out with her friends.

e I _____ (eat) so much ice-cream! I think I'm going to be sick.

f The trains _____ (run) late all morning.

g Sarah _____ (cry) all day because she _____ (fail) all her exams.

h I _____ (sunbathe) all morning, and now I'm bright red and very sore.

2 Present Perfect and Past Simple

T 2.1 Paul Cherry has had a long and varied career. Look at his picture and read about the events in his life. Complete the questions and answers.

Example
Where *was Paul born*? *In Leeds, Yorkshire.*

Age	**Paul Cherry**
0 –	Born Leeds, Yorkshire
11 –	Started Harrogate Grammar School, met best friend Julian
16 –	Moved to London
18 –	Sales representative for Candy Clothes Manufacturers
21 –	Married Maria, an Argentinian student
24 –	Moved to Argentina. Taught English
29 –	Son Peter born. Returned to England
32 –	Got a job as sales representative for Queen's English Publishers
34 –	Daughter Caroline born. Moved to detached house in Surrey
42 –	UK Manager for College Publishers
46 –	Made redundant
47 –	Met Julian again. Offered job as Marketing Director with Julian's company, Admiral Publishers
52 –	Admiral Publishers went bankrupt
55 –	Started market stall selling clothes
57 –	(now) Still selling clothes at Peckham market

a Which _____ to?
Harrogate Grammar School.

b How long _____ Julian?
Since _____ .

c How _____ to Maria?
For thirty-six years.

d What _____ in Argentina?
He _____ *English.*

e When _____ to England?
After _____ *born.*

f How many times _____ as a sales representative? *Twice.*

g Where _____ to after Caroline was born? *A house in Surrey.*

h How _____ clothes?
Since _____ .

i _____ Paul _____ a successful career?
No, he hasn't, because _____ .

Simple or continuous verb forms?

3 The world's highest dustman

1 **T 2.2** Read the text about David Clark. <u>Underline</u> the correct verb form. Sometimes both may be correct.

THE WORLD'S HIGHEST DUSTMAN

David Clark, 25, **(a)** *lives/is living* most of the time in York with his parents, but he is also the world's first mountaineering dustman. He **(b)** *has already been making/has already made* two trips to Mount Everest to collect rubbish left by expeditions there, and now he **(c)** *aims/'s aiming* to be the youngest person to climb the world's highest mountain.

It was while he **(d)** *worked/was working* in a climbing equipment shop that he **(e)** *heard/was hearing* about the rubbish left on Everest. He **(f)** *was looking/looked* for something really challenging to do and he liked the idea of being a dustman with a difference.

He is amazed at the type of junk he **(g)** *has found/has been finding*. At 17,000 ft he **(h)** *came/was coming* across cornflake packets, empty caviare tins, and hundreds of hypodermic needles and syringes. So far he **(i)** *has been collecting/has collected* enough rubbish to cover three football pitches.

For the last six months David **(j)** *has prepared/has been preparing* to climb to the summit of Everest. He **(k)** *'s training/trains* hard in the Himalayas and has been on a strict diet. If he **(l)** *succeeds/is succeeding* he will be the youngest British person ever to reach the top of Everest.

2 Read David's letter to his parents.
Fill the gaps with a verb from the box in the correct form. You need to decide which tense, and whether to use simple or continuous.

dream	think	sleep	be (×2)	check	do	try
learn	stay	mention	sunbathe	see	lie	tell
snow	make	get up	feel (×2)	begin	get	

Base Camp 1
Mt. Everest
July 28th

Dear Mum and Dad

I (a) _____ to feel quite nervous now about my climb to the top of Everest. However, I think I (b) _____ all that I can to prepare myself and I (c) _____ very fit, but is it enough? To be perfectly honest with you both, I am absolutely terrified.

As part of our training we (d) _____ how to survive in sub-zero conditions which (e) _____ (not) much fun. At night we (f) _____ in all kinds of strange places! Tonight we (g) _____ at the base camp. I often (h) _____ about my warm bed back home and Mum's cooking. I (i) _____ (not) you for four months now, but it (j) _____ like four years.

It's wonderful to get your letters and hear your news. I (k) _____ everyone here how hot it (l) _____ in England this summer, but they don't believe me. And I (m) _____ to imagine all the summer colours in our garden in York, because of course the only colour here is white. It (n) _____ a lot recently, so conditions are a little dangerous.

Today's a rest day. Some guys (o) _____, because believe it or not it gets very hot here around midday. Other people (p) _____ our equipment, which is a job we have to do all the time.

You (q) _____ in your last letter that you (r) _____ of selling the house. Please wait until I (s) _____ home before you (t) _____ any decisions. Our house is so beautiful, I'd be really upset if you sold it.

Anyway, it's 8 p.m., and my bedtime. I always (u) _____ at 4 a.m. so I'm usually in bed by 8.30 p.m. at the latest. I'd love (v) _____ in my bed at home right now. Anyway, I'm not!

Take care of yourselves.
Love
David

Passive

4 Present Perfect passive
Rewrite the newspaper headlines using the Present Perfect passive.

Example
Rat Alert at Buckingham Palace
*Rats **have been found** in Buckingham Palace.*

a **Dramatic Rescue of Yachtsman in Pacific**
_____
_____

b **Theft of Valuable Jewels from Harrods**
_____
_____

c ***MISSING BOY ALIVE***
_____

d **Huge Pay Rise for MPs**
_____

e **TORNADO KILLS 10 IN TEXAS**
_____

f **Ancient Tomb Discovery in Egypt**
_____

g **British Aerospace Shock – 2000 Redundancies**
_____

h **CURE FOR TEENAGE ACNE**
_____

5 *have* something *done*

> 1 *Have* something *done* = *have* + object + past participle.
> It is a passive structure.
> Notice the difference in meaning between these three sentences:
>
> > *I've repaired* my bicycle.
> > = I repaired it myself.
> >
> > *My bicycle* **has been repaired.**
> > = Someone repaired it. We are not interested who.
> >
> > *I've had* my bicycle **repaired.**
> > = I arranged/paid for someone to repair it for me.
>
> *have* + object + past participle
> It is often used to talk about services that you arrange to be done for you.
>
> > *I'm having* the kitchen **decorated.**
> > *I had* the house **painted.**
> > *I'm going to have* my hair **cut.**
>
> 2 *Get* something *done* can be used in a similar way, but not in the Present Perfect tense.
>
> > *I'm getting* the kitchen **decorated.**
> > *I'm going to get* my hair **cut.**

1 Rewrite the sentences using *have* something *done*.

Example
John's kitchen is being decorated.
He's *having the kitchen decorated.*

a One hundred copies of my report were printed.

I _____ .

b My sister wants someone to pierce her ears.

She wants to _____ .

c My eyes are going to be tested.

I'm going to _____ .

d Mr and Mrs Turner's leaking roof has been fixed.

They _____ .

e Our photocopier hasn't been mended yet.

We haven't _____ .

2 Melanie and Ken are getting married today.
Here are notes about some of their arrangements.

Recently	– cake decorated – wedding dress made – the invitations printed
Yesterday	– champagne delivered – hair cut – suit fitted – shirt pressed
Today	– hair done – nails manicured – feet massaged – photographs taken – bouquets delivered
Next week	– photos developed – wedding dress dry-cleaned

Who had/has had what done? Who is having what done? Make sentences about Melanie, Ken, or both of them, with the information in the chart.

She …
He …
They …

6 Transport

1 Put ticks (✔) to show which verbs go with which forms of transport.

	1 car	**2** bus	**3** train	**4** plane	**5** bicycle	**6** ferry
get into/out of	✔					
get on/off						
take off/land						
ride						
drive	✔					
catch/miss						
board						
overtake	✔					
park	✔					

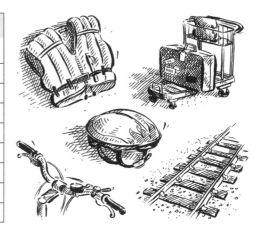

2 Put a number 1–6 next to the nouns in the box, depending on which type of transport they are associated with. Some can go into more than one category.

handlebars	runway	traffic lights	trolley	check-in desk	deck
one-way street	joyrider	life jacket	tyres	traffic jam	tunnel
slip road	trailer	ticket collector	track	spare tyre	lay-by
platform	jetty	service station	horn	timetable	porter
seat belt	carriage	season ticket	cargo	hand luggage	cabin
crash helmet	coach	gangway	port	Customs	

3 Read the clues and fill in the missing words in the puzzle. What is the vertical word?

a To go past another vehicle because you are moving faster (8)

b A home on wheels that is pulled by a car (7)

c A hard surface on which aircraft take off and land (6)

d A moveable bridge that people use for getting on or off a ship (7)

e A road that leads onto or off a motorway (4, 4)

f A person whose job is to carry suitcases at a railway station, airport, etc. (6)

g The goods that are carried in a ship or aircraft (5)

h A place where petrol and other goods are sold to motorists (7, 7)

i An underground passage, for example for a road or railway (6)

j The curved metal bar at the front of a bicycle that you hold when you are riding it (10)

k A journey to one or more places and back again, often by a different route (5, 4)

l A long line of cars, etc. that cannot move or that can only move very slowly (7, 3)

m The place where government officials check your luggage (7)

n Where you register as a passenger and weigh in your luggage at an airport (5-2, 4)

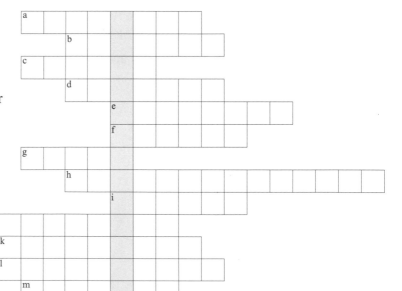

Prepositions

7 Prepositions of movement

Look at the pictures and read about Mary. Fill the gaps with a preposition from the list below. There may be several possibilities.

above	across	by
against	round	on
below	onto	down
along	beside	in
behind	off	into
up	out of	over
through	past	to
towards	at	

Mary's day out

The sun rose (**a**) ———— Mary's house. It was a beautiful day. Mary came (**b**) ———— her front door and went (**c**) ———— the path, (**d**) ———— the gate and (**e**) ———— the street. She crossed (**f**) ———— the road and walked (**g**) ———— the bus stop. The bus arrived and she got (**h**) ———— the bus. It went (**i**) ———— the corner, (**j**) ———— the High Street, (**k**) ———— all the shops and (**l**) ———— the countryside. It stopped (**m**) ———— the duck pond (**n**) ———— the next village, and Mary got (**o**) ————. She climbed (**p**) ———— a stile and started walking (**q**) ———— a big field. Suddenly, she saw a huge bull running (**r**) ———— her! She raced (**s**) ———— the far side of the field and squeezed (**t**) ———— the hedge. Out of breath, she sat down (**u**) ———— the grass (**v**) ———— the river. She leant back (**w**) ———— a rock. The sun was warm. Mary closed her eyes and listened to the water flowing (**x**) ————. Soon she was fast asleep. When she awoke the sun had disappeared (**y**) ———— the horizon.

Pronunciation

8 Word stress

1 **T 2.3** Look at the following pairs of words in phonetic script. They are all from Unit 2.

Notice where the stress marks are. Transcribe them and practise saying them aloud.

a /ɪkˈsplɔːrə/ /ˌekspləˈreɪʃən/ ———— ————
b /dʒəˈpæn/ /dʒæpəˈniːz/ ———— ————
c /ˈɒptɪmɪst/ /ɒptɪˈmɪstɪk/ ———— ————
d /ˈɪndəstrɪ/ /ɪnˈdʌstrɪəl/ ———— ————
e /ɪˈkɒnəmɪ/ /iːkəˈnɒmɪks/ ———— ————
f /ˈpɒlɪtɪks/ /pɒlɪˈtɪʃən/ ———— ————
g /ˈɒrɪdʒɪnz/ /əˈrɪdʒənəl/ ———— ————
h /ˈɒprə/ /ɒpəˈrætɪk/ ———— ————

2 What is the stress pattern of the words in Exercise 1? Write the words in the correct column.

● ●	● ●	● ● ●	● ● ●	● ● ●	● ● ● ●	● ● ● ●
		explorer			exploration	

3 **T 2.4** Read these words aloud. Write them in the correct column.

discovery	traveller	develop	backpacker	chocolates	photograph	religion
abroad	delicious	hotel	prehistoric	destruction	privileged	organize
inhabitant	unique	illegal	passenger	experiment	business	broadcast
overtake	caravan	create	photographer			

3 Narrative tenses
Time expressions

Irregular verbs

1 Past Simple and Past Perfect

1 Complete the sentences with the verb in **bold** in either the Past Simple or the Past Perfect. All the verbs are irregular.

fall ☐

a Harry _____ in love with a beautiful Greek girl while he was working in Athens.

b At last there was silence from the back of the car. All the children _____ asleep.

feel ☐

c She told me that she _____ sick with nerves before making that speech.

d Tom _____ really sorry for himself. Not only had his girlfriend gone off with his best friend, but he didn't get the promotion he wanted.

have ☐

e It was clear from the tense atmosphere that Susie and Gary _____ yet another row.

f We _____ breakfast on the veranda every morning whilst we were staying in Venice.

tear ☐

g Camilla _____ his letter into tiny pieces and threw it onto the fire.

h Johnny's mother asked him how he _____ his trousers.

cost ☐

i I didn't ask the price of Ted's new car, but I knew it _____ a fortune.

j It _____ more to have our word processor fixed than to buy a new one.

fly ☐

k My father _____ into a temper when he heard I'd failed my exams.

l I went to visit my brother in Australia. I was nervous because I _____ (never) before.

catch ☐

m We _____ a taxi outside the restaurant, and it took us to our hotel.

n She wondered how she _____ a cold in the middle of summer.

be ☐

o They _____ held hostage for over six weeks when they finally escaped.

p Talks _____ held in New York last week to discuss global warming.

2 Tick (✔) the verbs in Exercise 1 which have the same form for *both* the Past Simple and the past participle. Put a cross (✘) if they don't.

Past Simple, Past Continuous, Past Perfect

2 Past Simple or Past Continuous?

Underline the correct tense in the sentences.

Example
I *lived*/*was living* in Eastbourne when I *met*/*was meeting* my husband.

a Our team *played*/*was playing* really well. We *won*/*were winning* at half time, but in the end we *lost*/*were losing* 3–2.

b I'm worn out. The baby *was coughing*/*coughed* all night long and we *weren't getting*/*didn't get* any sleep.

c Jack *was playing*/*played* happily with his toys when his big brother *hit*/*was hitting* him on the head and *made*/*was making* him cry.

d I *didn't think*/*wasn't thinking* of having a birthday party, but now I'm glad I *had*/*was having* one.

e I *picked*/*was picking* two baskets of strawberries. I *gave*/*was giving* one basket to my neighbour and the rest I *made*/*was making* into jam.

f Roger *pruned*/*was pruning* the roses when he *heard*/*was hearing* a loud buzzing sound, and an enormous bee *appeared*/*was appearing* and *stung*/*was stinging* him on the nose.

g It *was snowing*/*snowed* when I *got up*/*was getting up* this morning. The children next door *made*/*were making* a snow man, so I quickly *put*/*was putting* on some warm clothes and *raced*/*was racing* outside to help them.

3 Past Simple or Past Perfect?

Put the verb in brackets in either the Past Simple or Past Perfect Simple.

Example
I *had* (have) an awful hangover because I *had drunk* (drink) too much the night before.

a I cooked a chicken curry for some friends, but I _____ (not find) out until the next day that I _____ (give) them all food poisoning.

b Sandra _____ (ring) her friend Dawn to ask about her holiday. Dawn _____ just _____ (return) from a cruise in the Caribbean.

c Since he was a little boy, Mark _____ (want) to go to Oxford University and study to become a doctor. Imagine his delight when he _____ (do) really well in all his exams! His childhood dream _____ (come) true.

d Kenneth _____ (have) a very difficult week. On Monday a water pipe _____ (burst) and flooded the kitchen, on Wednesday the central heating _____ (break) down, and on Friday his wife _____ (leave) him.

e Keith and Fiona _____ (go) to Brighton for their holiday last year. They _____ (be) there the year before and they _____ (have) an awful time, so I can't understand why they _____ (decide) to go back again.

f Rachel _____ (be) a successful model before she _____ (become) a teacher. She _____ (earn) a lot of money, but then she _____ (give) it all up for the classroom.

g Paul _____ (eat) so much chocolate pudding that his trousers _____ (not fit) him anymore.

h When I _____ (come) downstairs this morning, I couldn't believe my eyes. The children _____ (do) all the washing-up, and they _____ (make) breakfast for me.

4 Time expressions

1 In each group, complete a line (a–o) with a time expression (1–15). Use each expression once only.

a Sue gave up smoking _____

b Sue didn't give up smoking _____

c Sue hadn't given up smoking _____

d Sue had given up smoking _____

e Sue had been trying to give up smoking _____

1 for years.

2 when I first met her.

3 years ago.

4 until she was 30.

5 by the time she was thirty.

f Bill didn't wait _____

g Bill had been waiting _____

h Bill was waiting here _____

i Bill had been waiting an hour _____

j Bill waited _____

6 since six o'clock.

7 until I arrived.

8 when I finally arrived.

9 for long.

10 a minute ago.

k I haven't been feeling well _____

l They got on the plane _____

m I'd never seen him _____

n I was watching TV _____

o He didn't hear the attacker _____

11 until it was too late.

12 until late.

13 lately.

14 at the last minute.

15 before.

2 Complete these sentences, using the prompts in brackets.
   Use past tenses only and add any other words that are necessary.

a Two years ago, while I _____ .
   (work / Paris / grandfather / die)

b As soon as I _____ .
   (feed / cat / do / homework)

c First I _____ .
   (shower / then / dressed)

d Since I was a child I _____ always _____ .
   (want / Australia / finally / go / last year)

e As he _____ .
   (post / letter / realize / not put / stamp)

f By the time he'd _____ .
   (finish / speak / most / audience / fall asleep)

g Once I'd _____ .
   (tell him / truth / feel better)

h Until I _____ .
   (try water skiing / not believe / how difficult / be)

5 Puss in Boots

1 This is the true story of Jim and Rita Bell, and their cat, Whiskers. Look at the pictures and the verb phrases in the boxes below. Which words go with which pictures? Write the picture number next to the verbs.

Past Simple

- [ ] crashed into
- [ ] caught fire
- [ ] arrived
- [ ] pulled them out
- [ ] ran away
- [ ] knitted
- [ ] heard
- [ ] woke
- [ ] crept
- [ ] wore
- [ ] leapt up

Past Continuous

- [ ] were driving
- [ ] was miaowing
- [ ] was carrying
- [ ] the noise was coming from
- [ ] was lying awake
- [ ] were bleeding

Past Perfect

- [ ] had just waved
- [ ] had raced back
- [ ] hadn't found
- [ ] had found his way

Past Perfect Continuous

- [ ] had been staying
- [ ] had been dreaming
- [ ] had been walking

2 T 3.1 Complete the story about Jim and Rita Bell using the correct verb phrases from the boxes above.

PUSS IN BOOTS

Jim, Rita, and their cat, Whiskers **(a)** _____ home to London. They **(b)** _____ with their best friends Bob and Sue, in Edinburgh, and **(c)** _____ them goodbye. 700 kilometres of motorway lay ahead. Whiskers was not happy. He **(d)** _____ in his basket on the back seat. 'Poor Whiskers!' said Rita. 'Sh! Whiskers!' said Jim, 'I can't concentrate.' Suddenly there was a big bang, and Jim and Rita's car **(e)** _____ the car in front and **(f)** _____ . Fortunately, the police **(g)** _____ on the scene very soon and

(h) _____ of the car. However, poor Whiskers was left behind. Rita was distraught, and before the policeman could stop her, she **(i)** _____ to the burning car to save him. She **(j)** _____ Whiskers to safety in her arms, when suddenly there was a huge explosion. The cat **(k)** _____ into the air and **(l)** _____ . After an hour of fruitless search they still **(m)** _____ him, so with heavy hearts they set off again for home.

About two months passed. It was two o'clock in the morning and Rita **(n)** _____ in her bed in London. She **(o)** _____ about Whiskers. Suddenly she

(p) _____ a strange scratching sound. Thinking it might be burglars, she **(q)** _____ Jim up and quietly they **(r)** _____ downstairs. They couldn't tell where **(s)** _____ . Then Jim opened the front door and, to their amazement, there was Whiskers! He **(t)** _____ for over 60 days, and incredibly he **(u)** _____ home. He was exhausted and his paws **(v)** _____ , so Rita **(w)** _____ him some woollen, baby bootees, which he **(x)** _____ until his feet were better. So from then on he was called 'Puss in Boots'.

Past passives

6 Active to passive

In the following sentences the subject is either not important or too obvious to be necessary.

Put each sentence into the passive to make it sound more natural.

> **Example**
> Men were decorating my house all last week.
> My house *was being decorated all last week*.

a Archaeologists discovered a medieval temple underneath the new housing estate.

A medieval temple _____

_____ .

b The sports officials held the races indoors because it was raining.

The races _____

_____ .

c Burglars had broken into our house and stolen all my jewellery.

Our house _____

_____ .

d Someone had booked the leisure centre for a children's party on Saturday.

The leisure centre _____

_____ .

e The plumber was fixing the dishwasher so I couldn't leave the house.

The dishwasher _____

_____ .

f When we returned to our hotel room, the chambermaid still hadn't cleaned it.

Our hotel room _____

_____ .

g The chef hadn't cooked the fish for long enough. It was still raw!

The fish _____

_____ .

h Workmen were putting up new traffic lights at the crossroads.

New traffic lights _____

_____ .

3 **T 3.2** Complete the questions.

a Who _____ with?
   Bob and Sue.

b Why _____?
   Because he was unhappy in his basket in the car.

c What _____ their car?
   It crashed into the car in front and caught fire.

d What _____ when the car exploded?
   She was carrying Whiskers to safety.

e Why _____?
   Because the huge explosion frightened him.

f What _____?
   She'd been dreaming about Whiskers.

g How long _____?
   For over sixty days.

h Why _____?
   Because his paws were bleeding.

7 Here are some of the strangest deaths on record. Read these true stories and fill
the gaps with a verb from the right in the correct narrative tense, active or passive.

WHAT A WAY TO GO!

Maudie Walker
she died of excitement!

Maudie Walker was a 59-year-old contestant on a live American TV
quiz show, called *Temptation*. She (**a**) _____ (just)
in winning the game, and (**b**) _____ at the camera and
(**c**) _____ to all her family in the audience, when she
(**d**) _____ by the excitement of the moment and
(**e**) _____ a massive heart attack. She (**f**) _____ in
front of ten million viewers. *Temptation* has not been shown live since.

overcome

smile

succeed

suffer

die

wave

Major Summerfield
he was struck by lightning three times!

Major Summerfield was a victim of lightning three times, once even
after he (**a**) _____ . The first time was 1918. He
(**b**) _____ for the Canadian army in Flanders when he
(**c**) _____ by lightning and he (**d**) _____ off his horse.
However, he (e) _____ (not, badly).

Major Summerfield was a keen fisherman and six years later, back
in his home town of Vancouver, he (**f**) _____ and he
(**g**) _____ (just) a huge salmon, when lightning
(**h**) _____ again. This time it was more serious and his legs
(**i**) _____ .

He eventually died in 1932. On the day of his funeral there was a
terrible thunderstorm, and just as Major Summerfield
(**j**) _____ , lightning hit the graveyard, and his tombstone
(**k**) _____ into hundreds of tiny pieces.

bury

catch

die

fall

fight

fish

injure

paralyse

shatter

strike (×2)

Rueben Tice
he was killed by his own invention!

Rueben Tice was an electrician from Monterey, California but in his
spare time he was also an inventor. His first invention was an idea for
chilling cocktail glasses but this (**a**) _____ (not) very
successful.

In the winter of 1977, he (**b**) _____ on his latest invention.
This was an amazing device to take wrinkles out of prunes. He
(**c**) _____ (not) for six nights, because he (**d**) _____
the final touches to his great discovery. He was nearly ready to share it
with the world.

Unfortunately for mankind the machine (**e**) _____ with a
loud bang and Rueben (**f**) _____ on the head by a large metal
rod. He (**g**) _____ instantly. His dead body (**h**) _____
in thousands of prunes. Unfortunately they were still wrinkled!

be

cover

explode

hit

kill

put

sleep

work

8 The world of literature

The following words are related to either prose, poetry, or drama. Put them into the correct column(s). Some words fit two or all three categories.

Poetry	Prose	Drama

nursery rhyme
chapter
critic
backstage
science fiction
review
leading role
blockbuster
verse
scenery
rehearsal
standing ovation
ballad
performance
autobiography

plot
act
director
best-seller
script
character
novelist
fairy tale
props
whodunnit
stalls
hardback
thriller
playwright
paperback

9 Words commonly confused

These words are often confused. Fill the gaps with the correct word. Put the verbs into the correct forms.

1   expect   wait for   look forward to

a   We _____ the rain to stop so that we can play tennis.

b   The weather forecast says a lot of rain _____ over the next few days.

c   The children _____ opening their presents on Christmas Day.

2   floor   ground

a   The _____ was wet from all the rain.

b   We have tiled the _____ in our kitchen.

c   The Men's Department is on the _____ floor.

3   actually   at the moment   really

a   'What a shame James lost the match.'

    '_____, he won.'

b   The children are out playing in the garden _____ .

c   You _____ shouldn't have bothered.

4   alone   lone   lonely

a   I like living _____ , I never feel

    _____ .

b   A _____ survivor could be seen in the life raft.

5   ashamed   embarrassed   nervous

a   The actors were really _____ before the first performance.

b   He was _____ when his trousers split.

c   I feel so _____ . I shouldn't have lied.

6   bring   take   fetch

a   I _____ usually _____ to school by my father when I was a child.

b   My mother always _____ me back home.

c   Our dog can _____ sticks if you throw them for him.

7   see   watch   look at

a   _____ you _____ that new Spielberg film yet?

b   The police sat in their car. They _____ every move the men made.

c   _____ this lovely picture little Emma has painted!

Phrasal verbs

10 Type 1

There are four types of phrasal verbs. Type 1 is dealt with in this unit; types 2 and 3 are dealt with on page 41 in Unit 5; and type 4 is dealt with on page 55 of Unit 7.

⚠️

> Type 1 phrasal verbs consist of a verb + adverb.
> There is no object.
> They can be both literal and metaphorical.
>
> *She **stood up** and **walked out**.* (Literal)
> *Their marriage didn't **work out**, so they **broke up**.*
> (Metaphorical)

1   Match a phrasal verb in **A** with a definition in **B**.

A	B
show off	admit responsibility
find out	have a calmer, more stable life
doze off	explode
hold on	be quiet
speak up	discover
set off	be happier
blow up	not go out, stay at home
settle down	stop burning
turn up	arrive
own up	wait
cheer up	boast
go out	fall asleep
shut up	talk louder
stay in	begin a journey

2   Use one of the phrasal verbs in Exercise 1 to complete the sentences. Put the verb in the correct form.

a   Who broke the window? We aren't leaving this room until someone _____ .

b   The fire _____ because we didn't put enough wood on it.

c   'Is Peter at the party?'

'No, but I'm sure he _____ soon.'

d   We have a long journey tomorrow. What time do we have to _____?

e   Why are you so miserable? _____! It's not the end of the world.

f   'I came first in all my exams.'

'Stop _____! You're such a big head.'

g   I don't feel like going out tonight. Shall we _____?

h   Larry was a bit wild at university, but then he got a job, found a lovely wife, _____ and had kids.

i   After a heavy meal and a glass or two of wine, I _____ in front of the telly.

j   Can I copy your homework? The teacher will never _____ .

k   _____! I'm trying to watch a programme and you're all talking.

l   'What's Bill's phone number?'

'_____ . I'll just look in my address book.'

m   _____! We can't hear you at the back!

n   A soldier was injured when the bridge he was crossing _____ .

11 Diphthongs

> ⚠️ Diphthongs are two vowel sounds which run together.
>
> **hear** /hɪə/ = /ɪ/ + /ə/ diphthong /ɪə/   **hair** /heə/ = /e/ + /ə/ diphthong /eə/
>
> There is a list on the inside back cover of this Workbook.

1   T 3.3   Circle the correct transcription of the word.

a pay   (peɪ)   /peə/   d round /reɪnd/ /raʊnd/   g tour /tʊə/ /təʊ/
b write /raɪt/ /rəʊt/   e dear   /dɪə/   /deə/   h fair /fɪə/ /feə/
c phone /fəʊn/ /faɪn/   f boy   /bəʊ/   /bɔɪ/

2   T 3.4   All these words in phonetic script contain diphthongs. Transcribe them.

a /nɪə/ _____   d /flaɪt/ _____   g /taʊn/ _____

b /keə/ _____   e /peɪdʒ/ _____   h /fjʊə/ _____

c /θrəʊ/ _____   f /dʒɔɪn/ _____

3   T 3.5   Read the poem aloud. Write the number next to the correct sound.

Sounds and letters don't agree

When the English tongue we speak,
Why does (**1**) *break* not rhyme with (**2**) *weak*?   **2** /iː/   **1** /eɪ/
Won't you tell me why it's true
We say (**3**) *sew*, but also (**4**) *few*?   ☐ /uː/   ☐ /əʊ/
And the maker of a verse
Cannot rhyme his (**5**) *horse* with (**6**) *worse*?   ☐ /ɔː/   ☐ /ɜː/
(**7**) *Beard* is not the same as (**8**) *heard*.   ☐ /ɜː/   ☐ /ɪə/
(**9**) *Cord* is different from (**10**) *word*,   ☐ /ɜː/   ☐ /ɔː/
(**11**) *Cow* is cow, but (**12**) *low* is low,   ☐ /aʊ/   ☐ /əʊ/
(**13**) *Shoe* is never rhymed with (**14**) *foe*.   ☐ /uː/   ☐ /əʊ/
Think of (**15**) *hose* and (**16**) *dose* and (**17**) *lose*,   ☐ /uːz/   ☐ /əʊz/   ☐ /əʊs/
And think of (**18**) *loose* and yet of (**19**) *choose*,   ☐ /uːz/   ☐ /uːs/
Think of (**20**) *comb* and (**21**) *tomb* and (**22**) *bomb*   ☐ /ɒm/   ☐ /uːm/   ☐ /əʊm/
(**23**) *Doll* and (**24**) *roll* and (**25**) *home* and (**26**) *some*.   ☐ /ɒl/   ☐ /əʊl/   ☐ /ʌm/   ☐ /əʊm/
And since (**27**) *pay* is rhymed with (**28**) *say*   ☐ /eɪ/
Why not (**29**) *paid* with (**30**) *said* I pray?   ☐ /eɪ/   ☐ /e/
Think of (**31**) *blood* and (**32**) *food* and (**33**) *good*;   ☐ /ʊ/   ☐ /uː/   ☐ /ʌ/
(**34**) *Mould* is not pronounced like (**35**) *could*.   ☐ /ʊd/   ☐ /əʊld/
Why is it (**36**) *done*, but (**37**) *gone* and (**38**) *lone*   ☐ /əʊ/   ☐ /ʌ/   ☐ /ɒ/
Is there any reason known?
To sum up, it seems to me
That sounds and letters don't agree.

Countable and uncountable nouns
Expressing quantity
something, *somebody*, *somewhere*
all and *every*

Countable and uncountable nouns

1 Countable or uncountable?

Underline the noun that is usually uncountable in each group. Use your dictionary to look up any new words.

Example
shirt <u>fashion</u> skirt tie blouse

a holiday journey flight luggage suitcase

b meal dish food menu dessert

c cheque coin cash salary bonus

d tractor corn barn field orchard

e raspberry plum fruit fig mango

f job employee boss unemployment profession

g basement attic cellar bedsit accommodation

h health pill disease operation prescription

i disco musical music opera concert

j motorway traffic traffic jam lorry rush hour

Expressing quantity

2 *some* or *any*?

Complete the sentences with *some* or *any*.

a I did Exercise 1 without _____ help.

b Would you like _____ more fizzy mineral water?

I don't want _____ more.

c _____ people don't have _____ problems learning foreign languages.

d Why don't you ask your father to lend you _____

money? I haven't got _____ .

e My teenage sister never has _____ trouble learning the words of the latest pop songs. There are hardly

_____ she doesn't know by heart.

f I didn't realize that there were still _____

sandwiches left. I've made _____ more.

3 *much* or *many*?

Rewrite the sentences using the words in brackets and *much* or *many*. Make any other necessary changes.

Example
I'm not sure how much drink to buy. (cans of beer)
I'm not sure how many cans of beer to buy.

a Are there many jobs to be done in the garden? (work)

_____

_____

b I didn't spend many hours on the homework. (time)

_____

_____

c Did they do many experiments before they found a cure? (research)

_____

_____

d They couldn't give me many details about the delay in our flight. (information)

_____

_____

e There are too many cars and lorries on the streets of our town. (traffic)

_____

_____

f I didn't have too much difficulty with this exercise. (problems)

_____

_____

4 The canteen

1 Look at the picture of the students' canteen.
Write ten sentences about it.
Use each expression in the box at least once.

several	a couple of	a few	isn't much
lots of	aren't many	a little	hardly any
no	a huge amount of		

a _____

b _____

c _____

d _____

e _____

f _____

g _____

h _____

i _____

j _____

2 **T 4.1** Answer the students' questions.
Use an expression of quantity **without** a noun.

Examples
Is there any chocolate cake?
Sorry, there's _none_ left/there _isn't any_.

What about rice?
Well, there's _a little_.

a Can I have some spaghetti?

Yes, of course, there _____ .

b Have you got lots of ham sandwiches?

Well, there are _____ .

c I'd like two vegetable curries, please.

Sorry, there _____ left.

d Can I have some chips with my hamburger?

Sorry, there _____ .

e Have you got apple pie today?

Yes, just _____ .

f Are there any chocolate biscuits?

Well, there _____ .

g Can I have a large portion of fruit salad, please?

Sorry, there _____ left.

h Are there any bananas left?

Yes, I think we _____ .

i Is this all the apple juice you've got?

Yes, I'm afraid there's only _____ .

j Well, I'll have some grapefruit juice.

No problem, we've got _____ .

5 very little, a little, very few, a few, fewer, less

Rewrite the sentences with *very little*, *a little*, *very few*, *a few*, *fewer*, or *less*. Change all the words underlined.

Example
There was a lot of wine at the party, but <u>hardly any</u> was drunk.
There was a lot of wine at the party, but *very little* was drunk.

a I'm on a diet so I'll just have <u>four or five</u> chips.

_____

_____

b I'll have a <u>drop of</u> whisky, just to help me sleep.

_____

_____

c Children <u>don't</u> have <u>as much</u> respect for their teachers <u>as</u> they used to.

_____

_____

d Lots of people have tried to climb Everest, but <u>not many</u> have succeeded.

_____

_____

e Dave can speak fluent Norwegian and <u>some</u> Swedish.

_____

_____

f <u>Not as many</u> people smoke these days.

_____

g <u>Not many</u> people manage to become completely fluent in a language.

_____

h It's been <u>two or three</u> years since we last saw him.

_____

_____

i There <u>isn't</u> very <u>much</u> I can do to help you.

_____

j There are lots of reasons why I don't want to marry you. Here are <u>some</u> of them.

_____

_____

6 From riches to rags

from RICHES

Fred Corbett lives in a hostel for the homeless and sells as (**a**) _____ copies of the *Big Issue* (a magazine by homeless people) as he can. He earns about £30 a week, which is (**b**) _____ money. Yet only (**c**) _____ years ago Fred was a millionaire, living the good life. What went wrong? He tells us his story:

'When I was 18 years old my parents died in a car accident and I inherited (**d**) _____ of money. I had (**e**) _____ other family, and very (**f**) _____ friends and so there was (**g**) _____ I could really talk to about my grief. The only thing that seemed to help was spending money. When people learned how (**h**) _____ money I had, they became really friendly. I began to realize that (**i**) _____ people only liked me for my money.

'I bought a helicopter and (**j**) _____ cars, but I crashed (**k**) _____ of them. So on the advice of my accountant I bought (**l**) _____ of shares in Barings Bank. Maybe you can guess what happened next. Barings Bank went bankrupt, and I lost a fortune. I had (**m**) _____ money

1 Look at the pictures and read the story of Fred Corbett. Fill the gaps with words from the box. Careful! You can use each word or phrase **once** only.

many	no	several	a couple	fewer
less	much	a large number	very little	a few
few	all	a huge amount	anything	nobody
most	none	hardly any	something	a lot

2 The following sentences contain false information. Correct the mistakes.

Example
Most people think that £30 a week is a lot of money.
Very few/Not many people think that £30 a week is a lot of money.

a Fred has few relatives.

_____

b Fred talked to his friends about his grief.

_____

to RAGS

left, just a couple of hundred pounds, so of course I now had far (**n**) _____ friends because I had much (**o**) _____ money. When I finally ran out of money, (**p**) _____ of my so-called friends stood by me, so I was friendless, homeless, and penniless.

'It's difficult to believe, but I'm (**q**) _____ happier now that I'm so poor. I've made (**r**) _____ of real friends at the hostel, Ken and Dave, and that's more important to me than (**s**) _____ else. (**t**) _____ I've learned from my experience is that money can't buy you love!'

c People were friendly to Fred because he had lost his parents.

_____

_____

d He invested very little of his money.

_____

e Fred didn't have any money left when Barings went bankrupt.

_____

_____

f A few friends helped Fred when he ran out of money.

_____

g Fred has never made any real friends.

_____

h Fred hasn't learned anything from his experience.

_____

Compounds with *some, any, no, every*

7 *something, anybody, everyone, nowhere ...*

1 *Any, anyone, anybody, anywhere,* and *anything* can mean *it doesn't matter which/ who/ where/ what.*

   Put the picture **anywhere**, I don't mind.
   You can say **anything** you want. I don't care.
   Borrow **any** book you want.

2 *Everybody* and *everything* are singular, not plural.

   Everybody **knows** who did it.
   Everything **is** ready for the party.

1 Complete the following sentences with a combination of these words.

some	
any	one
no	+ body
	thing
every	where

a I don't care where we go on holiday as long as it's _____ hot.

b Does _____ want a cup of tea?

c I've looked _____ for my contact lens, but I can't find it _____ .

d 'What do you want for dinner Harry?'
   'Oh, _____, I don't care!'

e This sale is fantastic. There's 50% off _____ in the shop.

f It's really boring at Auntie Martha's, there's absolutely _____ to do.

g I'm a very sensitive person. _____ understands me.

h I'll go _____ as long as I'm with you.

i Jane's getting married to _____ she met on holiday.

j Sue is such a chatterbox, she's always got _____ to say but she never says _____ interesting.

k Our dog will go for a walk with _____ .

l Tommy's so nice. _____ likes him.

2 Match a line in **A** with a line in **B**.

A	B
a He told the police that he knew He didn't tell the police	anything. nothing.
b I think they live I don't mind. I'll live	anywhere in London. somewhere in London.
c Anybody Nobody	phoned you. Sorry. can cook. It's easy.
d I've searched I can't find it	anywhere. everywhere.
e I thought I'd know I didn't know	somebody at the party. anyone at the party.
f My parents never took me My parents took me	everywhere when I was young. anywhere when I was a kid.
g Jane always got Jane didn't have	everything she wanted. anything to wear.
h I've already had I've had	something to eat. nothing to eat.

all and *every*

1 *Every* is used with singular, countable nouns.
All is used with countable nouns in the plural and uncountable nouns in the singular.

> ***Every flower*** in the garden **is** beautiful.
> ***All the flowers*** in the garden **are** beautiful.
> ***All flowers are*** beautiful.
> ***All housework is*** dull.

2 We do not usually use *all* to mean *everybody/everyone/everything*.

> ***Everybody*** had a good time.   *~~All had~~ ...~~
> ***Everything*** was ruined in the fire.   *~~All was~~ ...~~
> I said hello to ***everyone***.

However, if *all* is followed by a relative clause, it can mean *everything*.

> ***All*** (that) I own is yours.
> I spend ***all*** I earn.
> My uncle left me ***everything*** in his will.
> My uncle left me ***everything/all he owned***.

3 This structure can have a negative meaning, expressing ideas such as *nothing more* or *only this*.

> ***All I want*** is a place to sleep.
> ***All*** he left me was his umbrella.
> ***All*** you need is love.

8 *all* or *every*?

Underline the correct answer.

a Anna is such a show-off, she thinks she knows *all/everything*.

b My driving test was a complete disaster. *All/Everything* went wrong.

c Kate didn't say where she was going. *All/Everything* she said was that she was going out.

d *All/Every* child in the class failed the exam.

e *All/Everything* those children need is a bit of discipline, then they wouldn't be so naughty.

f *All/Everything* I want for my birthday is to lie in bed until midday.

g I'm starving. *All/Everything* I've eaten today is a packet of crisps.

h We both work full-time, but my husband never lifts a finger. He expects me to do *all the/every* housework.

i I really don't get on with my new boss. I disagree with *all/everything* she says.

j I can't go higher than £500 for the car. That's *everything/all* I can afford.

k Megan couldn't believe her luck. *All/Every* topic she had revised the night before came up in the exam.

Vocabulary

9 A piece of cake!

1 What combinations can you make using nouns from the two boxes?

a	jar slice tube loaf bar box tin can piece bottle sheet	of	bread honey cake soap toothpaste soup beer chocolate chocolates paper Coke

2 Replace the words in italics with combinations from Exercise 1.

a Would you like *some cake*?

_____

b All we've got for lunch is *some soup*.

_____

c There are two clean *pieces of paper* on my desk.

_____

d Don't forget to buy Mum *some chocolates* for Mother's Day.

_____

e Do you want this *chocolate*? It's plain and I only like milk.

_____

f There's only one *bit of bread* in the bread bin.

_____

g How *much beer* have we got left over from the barbecue?

_____

h Hello reception? This is room 401. There's not a single *bit of soap* in the bathroom here. Can some be sent up, please?

_____

i We brought you *some* special apple blossom *honey* back from the country.

_____

Prepositions

10 Prepositions and nouns

1 Which prepositions go with the words on the right?

A

above	below	on	over	under	
✓	✓	✓			average
					foot
					arrest
					£500
					75%
					freezing
					18 years old
					new management
					holiday
					pressure
					business

B

at	by	during	in	on	
✓	✓				midnight
					the night
					New Year's Day
					the winter
					Friday afternoon
					the weekend
					time
					a fortnight's time
					the rush hour
					his forties

2 **T 4.2** Complete the article with the correct preposition. Some are from Exercise 1 on page 33.

Teenage Football Wonder!

Tony Zucci of Manchester Rovers is the most famous young footballer in the UK. He has scored **(a)** _____ 40 goals this season and was voted footballer of the year, and he's still only **(b)** _____ his teens.

Two years ago Tony was **(c)** _____ holiday with his parents **(d)** _____ a Spanish seaside resort. He was playing football **(e)** _____ the beach with some local boys when football manager Chris Hill, who was there **(f)** _____ business, spotted him. **(g)** _____ the end of the holiday, Tony had signed his first contract for Manchester Rovers.

Tony works hard to keep fit. **(h)** _____ Mondays, Wednesdays, and Fridays he gets up **(i)** _____ dawn for training. Even **(j)** _____ the winter months, when the temperature is often **(k)** _____ freezing, he never misses a session.

Manchester Rovers now have a five-point lead in the Premier Division, and they are **(l)** _____ a lot of pressure to be the first team to win the cup for the third year **(m)** _____ succession.

We shall know the outcome of the championship **(n)** _____ the end of next week, but with Tony Zucci, star striker, **(o)** _____ the team my money's definitely on Manchester Rovers.

11 Sentence stress

T 4.3 Alan and Kevin are gossiping about Frank, who is a mutual friend. Read the sentences aloud and mark the main stressed word or words in **B**'s responses.

Example
A Don't you think Frank's put on a lot of weight recently?
●   ●   ●
B You're kidding. If anything, he's lost weight.

a **A** I think Frank earns more than me.

  B Well, I know he earns a lot more than me.

b **A** He's thinking of buying a second-hand Mercedes.

  B What do you mean? He's already bought a brand new one.

c **A** He's just bought two pairs of designer jeans.

  B Didn't you know that all Frank's clothes are designer labels?

d **A** Does Frank have many stocks and shares?

  B He has loads of them.

e **A** Isn't Frank in New York on business?

  B No, in fact he's in Florida on holiday.

f **A** His latest girlfriend has long, blonde hair.

  B Really? The girl I saw him with had short, brown hair.

12 Phonetics – fruit or vegetable?

1 Transcribe these words from phonetic script and write them in the correct column.

/kærət/	/kɒlɪflaʊə/	/greɪpfruːt/	/peə/	/pəteɪtəʊ/
/paɪnæpl/	/tʃərɪ/	/kæbɪdʒ/	/liːk/	/melən/
/ɒrɪndʒ/	/kʊəʒet/	/pɑːsnɪp/	/plʌm/	/strɔːbərɪ/
/kjuːkʌmbə/	/rɑːzbərɪ/	/ævəkɑːdəʊ/	/piː/	/mæŋgəʊ/
/swɪːtkɔːn/	/spɪnɪtʃ/	/ʌnjən/		

Fruit	Vegetables

2 **T 4.4** Mark the stress and practise saying the words aloud.

Future forms
Conjunctions in time clauses

Future forms

1 Question tags

Match a sentence in **A** with a question tag in **B**.

A	B
a You're going to work harder from now on,	will we?
b I'll see you next week,	doesn't it?
c Kate's leaving soon,	won't we?
d You'll ring when you get there,	are you?
e Our plane takes off at 4 p.m.,	won't I?
f The decorators will have finished by next week,	isn't she?
g You aren't getting married next week,	won't you?
h We won't need tickets to get in,	won't they?
i We'll be millionaires one day,	will he?
j Max won't be coming,	aren't you?

2 *will* or *going to*?

T 5.1 Complete the following sentences using *will* or *going to* in the correct form. Sometimes both *will* and *going to* are possible.

a **A** I _____ make myself a sandwich. Do you want one?

   B No thanks. I _____ have something later.

b **A** Helen and Les _____ Florida this year for their holidays.

   B How wonderful! The boys _____ love it, especially Disneyland.

c **A** Bye, Mum. I _____ meet Tom and

   Mel. I _____ be back at about ten o'clock.

   B Have a good time, but don't be late again or

   I _____ be furious.

d **A** Jo _____ be mad with me when she finds out I've smashed the car.

   B She _____ understand. Just tell her it wasn't your fault.

e **A** I (not) _____ work today, I feel awful.

   B Don't worry, I _____ ring your boss and tell her you're sick.

f **A** I'm tired. I think I _____ go to bed.

   B Goodnight. I _____ watch the news,

   then I _____ join you.

g **A** My boss has told me I _____ be promoted. I'm afraid that means longer hours at the office, darling.

   B Don't worry. I _____ get myself a dog for

   company. I'm sure we _____ have more to talk about!

h **A** Mr Smith, now you've won the lottery you

   _____ be the fifth richest man in England. How do you feel about that?

   B I _____ tell you next week. I'm too overwhelmed to think about it now.

3 What does John say?

Complete what John actually says using a future form. Sometimes there are several possibilities.

Example
He sees some very black clouds in the sky.
John: 'It*'s going to rain*.'

a His sister has just reminded him that it is his grandmother's birthday soon.

John: 'I _____ .'

b He has decided to study hard for his final exams.

John: 'I _____ .'

c He's made an appointment to see the dentist next Friday.

John: 'I _____ .'

d He predicts a win for his team, Manchester United, on Saturday.

John: 'I think _____

_____ .'

e He's stuck in a traffic jam. He's late for a meeting. He rings his office.

John: 'I'm sorry. _____ .'

f His sister is pregnant. The baby is due next March.

John: 'My sister _____

_____ .'

g His plane ticket for next Sunday says:
Departure 7.30 a.m. London, Heathrow.

John: 'My plane _____

_____ .'

h He can see himself lying on a beach in Spain next week at this time.

John: 'I _____

_____ .'

4 Future Continuous or Future Perfect?

Ann's very ambitious. These are the things she believes she *will be doing* or *will have done* by the time she's forty. Put each resolution into either the Future Continuous or Future Perfect.

Example
buy a Rolls Royce   *I'll have bought a Rolls Royce.*
work in America   *I'll be working in America.*

a become a multi-millionaire

_____

b run my own computer business

_____

c move to California

_____

d live in a mansion in Beverly Hills

_____

e join a highly exclusive tennis club

_____

f marry a handsome actor

_____

g earn over £2,000,000 a year

_____

h give up smoking

_____

5 A Hollywood interview

1 **T 5.2** Underline the appropriate future form. Sometimes both are possible.

Third time lucky for Hollywood's most celebrated couple

HOLLYWOOD STARS Selina Sullivan, 37, and Ricardo Sanchez, 35, (a) *are getting/will be getting* **married next month, in the celebrity wedding of the year. What makes this ceremony extra special for Selina and Ricardo is that this is the third time they (b)** *are exchanging/will have exchanged* **wedding vows. They have been married to each other twice before!**

'Hot Gossip' magazine asked Selina and Ricardo some questions about their forthcoming wedding and their plans for their future together as man and wife (again!).

■ *Selina, what are your thoughts about your marriage to Ricardo next month, and why have you decided to make this wedding such a grand and public affair?*

S This is the last time I **(c)** *make/'ll make* my marriage vows. I know now that I am fully committed to Ricardo and our future together. Before, I was too immature to appreciate what a caring and loving man Ricardo is. This time we **(d)** *'ll tell/are going to tell* the world about our love and that is why we **(e)** *'ll have/are having* such a big wedding.

■ *Ricardo,* **(f)** *will you invite/will you be inviting* your family this time? You've always excluded them from your previous weddings to Selina.

R All my family from Spain **(g)** *will come/are coming* this time. Mama and Papa **(h)** *will arrive/will have arrived* from Madrid one week before the ceremony so that they can really get to know Selina again.

■ *I've heard that over 300 guests will be at your wedding and that the President and his wife have been invited. Is this true?*

2 Do you think that Selina and Ricardo will have a happy future together? Complete the sentences, putting the verb in brackets in an appropriate future form!

What happens next? This time next year I think …

a Selina ⎯⎯⎯⎯⎯⎯⎯⎯⎯⎯ (expect) a baby.

b They ⎯⎯⎯⎯⎯⎯⎯⎯⎯⎯ (own) an even bigger house in LA.

c Selina ⎯⎯⎯⎯⎯⎯⎯⎯⎯⎯ (fall) out with Ricardo's parents.

d Selina and Ricardo ⎯⎯⎯⎯⎯⎯⎯⎯⎯⎯ (have) lots of arguments.

e Ricardo ⎯⎯⎯⎯⎯⎯⎯⎯⎯⎯ (work) on his latest blockbuster film.

f Selina ⎯⎯⎯⎯⎯⎯⎯⎯⎯⎯ (worry) about losing her figure because of the baby.

g Ricardo ⎯⎯⎯⎯⎯⎯⎯⎯⎯⎯ (not remember) their wedding anniversary.

h Selina ⎯⎯⎯⎯⎯⎯⎯⎯⎯⎯ (want) to get divorced for the third time.

i They ⎯⎯⎯⎯⎯⎯⎯⎯⎯⎯ (not agree) to give another interview to *Hot Gossip*.

S Yes. About 300 of our very closest friends and family **(i)** *are coming/will come*. Ricardo and I have known the President and his wife for many years, but unfortunately they **(j)** *won't come/won't be coming* as they have another engagement on that day.

■ *Ricardo, could you tell us what you have planned for the ceremony?*

R We **(k)** *will have/are going to have* a twilight ceremony beneath a canopy of white roses at my Spanish-style villa here in LA. The ceremony **(l)** *won't start/doesn't start* until 9 p.m., but guests **(m)** *will arrive/will be arriving* at 7 p.m. for a light champagne supper before the wedding begins.

■ *And the honeymoon?*

R That's my wedding present to Selina and it's a surprise. All she knows is that we have a flight booked on Concorde. It **(n)** *is going to leave/leaves* at 11.30 p.m. the following day from New York.

S Ricardo is so romantic, it's one of the many reasons why I love him. Also he adores children and this time we want to start a family. I know that if we have a child he **(o)** *'ll be/is going to be* a marvellous father.

■ *On behalf of 'Hot Gossip' magazine I'd like to wish you all the best for the future.*

6 Correcting mistakes

In the following dialogues some of the future forms are wrong. Find the mistakes and correct them.

Example

✓ **A** Have you heard? Sue's going to have a baby.

          I'll

✗ **B** Really? ~~I'm going to~~ give her a ring this evening to congratulate her.

a ☐ **A** What do you do this weekend?

  ☐ **B** I don't know yet. Maybe I'll give Paul a ring and see what he's doing.

b ☐ **A** I'll be honest with you, Matthew. I don't think you're going to pass this exam.

  ☐ **B** Oh, no! What will I be doing?

c ☐ **A** Is it true that Rachel will get married to that awful boyfriend of hers this weekend?

  ☐ **B** I'm afraid so. And I'm going to the wedding. I've got to. I'm her bridesmaid!

d ☐ **A** Our plane leaves at six o'clock on Saturday morning.

  ☐ **B** Yuk! You have to wake me up. I can never get up in the mornings.

e ☐ **A** It's my birthday on Sunday. I'm going to be 30!

  ☐ **B** Thirty! That's ancient! You are getting your pension soon.

f ☐ **A** Mickey and David will be arriving soon, and the house looks like a pigsty.

  ☐ **B** Don't worry. It'll only be taking a few minutes to clear up.

g ☐ **A** Will you be going skiing as usual after Christmas?

  ☐ **B** Not this year. It's too expensive. We'll stay at home.

h ☐ **A** I'll ring you as soon as I'll arrive.

  ☐ **B** Please do. We'll be waiting to hear you've arrived safely.

Conjunctions in time clauses

7 Future time clauses

1 Notice that in clauses after *if*, *when*, *as soon as*, *until*, *before*, *after*, *once*, and *unless* present tenses are normally used to talk about the future. A future form is *not* used.

    I'll phone you **when I arrive**.   *when I 'll arrive*

    I won't marry you **unless you give up** smoking!

    unless you'll give up

2 If it is important to show that the first action will be completed before the second action begins, the Present Perfect is used.

    I'll fax you the report **as soon as I've written** it.

    They're going to emigrate to Australia **after the baby has been born**.

Put the verbs in brackets in the correct tense, Present Simple, Present Perfect, or a future form.

a You _____ (not get) better unless you _____ (eat) sensibly.

b We _____ (not move) to Paris until we _____ (find) a flat there to rent.

c You _____ (love) Adam when you _____ (meet) him. He's so funny.

d _____ you _____ (learn) to drive as soon as you _____ (be) 17?

e The children _____ (not go) to bed unless they _____ (have) a glass of milk.

f It _____ (be) at least an hour before I _____ (finish) this report.

g If you _____ (not do) well in the test, _____ you _____ (have to) do it again?

h We _____ (deal) with your request as soon as we _____ (be) able to process the information.

i The doctor says that I _____ (feel) much better once I _____ (have) the operation.

j Once you _____ (try) 'Glowhite' toothpaste, you _____ (never use) anything else!

Vocabulary

8 Health

Use your dictionary to check new words.

1 Match a person in **A** with suitable lines from **B** and **C**.
  Make at least one sentence about each person.

   Example
   The nurse took the patient's temperature.

A	B	C
The nurse	performed	his knee.
The surgeon	suffered	her wrist.
The accident victim	had	in the smoky atmosphere.
The toddler	took	during the crossing.
The teenager	fell over and grazed	the patient's temperature.
The pregnant woman	felt faint	a difficult operation.
The old man	felt sea-sick	in the attack.
The tennis player	sprained	on a stretcher.
The racing driver	was wounded	a heart attack.
The soldier	was carried	from sunburn.
The gardener	was stung	the crash.
The ferry passengers	was lucky to survive	by a wasp.
The holidaymaker		spots on her face.

2 Choose the word or phrase which best completes the sentences.

a wounded   injured   damaged

Footballer Jimmie White was _____ in the
second half of the match in a tackle with the
goalkeeper.

b sprained   sore   dislocated

He'll be out of the game for several weeks with a
_____ shoulder.

c a bandage   stitches   a sling

My daughter fell off her bike and she had to have
_____ in her leg.

d pain   ache   indigestion

Suddenly Tom felt a sharp _____ in his
stomach.

e bruises   a rash   warts

Whenever I eat shellfish I get _____ all over
my body.

f allergic to   allergic with   allergic from

Lots of people are _____ shellfish.

g a blister   a blemish   a boil

Ouch! I've got _____ on my heel from
these new shoes.

h drowsy   tipsy   dizzy

My husband hates heights. When he looks down he
feels _____ .

i run in   run over   run down

There's nothing seriously wrong with me. I'm just a

bit _____ because I've been working so
hard recently.

j damages   hurts   injures

There's no doubt about it. Smoking _____
your health.

9 Hot Verbs *be* and *have*

1 Which words and expressions go with *be*, and which go with *have*? Tick the correct column.

be		have
✓	fed up with sb/sth	
	a right to do sth	✓
	the nerve to do sth	
	on the safe side	
	in touch with sb	
	sb round	
	a word with sb	
	no point in doing sth	
	off colour	
	on one's mind	
	out of one's mind	
	up to date	
	a ball	
	in charge of sb/sth	
	no chance of doing sth	

2 Complete the sentences with one of the expressions above in the correct form.

Examples
My job is so boring. I*'m* really *fed up with* it.
If you don't like your meal, you *have* every *right* to complain.

a There aren't usually any major side-effects after this injection, but you might _____ a bit _____ for a few days.

b Thank you for your time, Miss Clarke. We still have to interview a few more candidates, so we _____ with you as soon as we've made a decision.

c We _____ Mel and Andy_____ for dinner next Friday. We haven't seen them for ages.

d I can't stop thinking about my ex-girlfriend. She _____ always _____ .

e Where have you been all night? I _____ _____ with worry. I even rang the police.

f Excuse me, Mrs Bennett! Can I _____ _____ for a minute? It's about your son Ben.

g Jack was so cheeky! He _____ to tell me that I was too fat. He should look at himself in the mirror!

h I've got extra insurance just in case we have an accident on holiday. You know me! I always like _____ .

i I'm going to apply for a new job, but I know I _____ getting it. I just don't have the right experience.

j I _____ the office while the manager is away for a few days.

k Did you read Sally's postcard? She's in Greece, sunbathing all day and dancing all night. It sounds like she's _____ .

l If there's something you don't like, it's just bad luck. There _____ complaining. It's the same for all of us.

m If you're a stock broker, you need to _____ on the state of the markets in different parts of the world.

Phrasal verbs

10 Types 2 and 3

> ⚠️
>
> 1 Both type 2 and type 3 phrasal verbs have an object.
>
> **Type 2**
> *Take off **your coat**.*
> *I didn't want to let **my friends** down.*
>
> **Type 3**
> *Look after **your sister**.*
> *I can always get round **my father**.*
>
> 2 In type 2, the particle can move.
> *Take your coat **off**.*
> *I didn't want to let **down** my friends.*
>
> If the object is a pronoun (*him*, *it*, *me*, etc.) the particle comes after it.
> *Take it **off**.*   *~~Take off it.~~*
> *I didn't want to let **them** down*   *~~to let down them~~*
>
> 3 In type 3, the particle cannot move.
> *~~Look your sister after.~~*
> *~~Look her after.~~*
> *I can always ~~get my father round.~~*
> *I can always ~~get him round.~~*
>
> 4 Dictionaries tell you which type a phrasal verb is.
> **make sth up** The particle is shown after **sth**. This is type 2.
> **look into sth** The particle is shown before **sth**. This is type 3.

Put a pronoun in the correct place in these sentences. To do this, you need to decide which type of phrasal verbs is being used.

Examples
The music is too loud. Please turn _it_ down _____ .
I know you've got a lot of problems, but I'm sure you'll come _____ through _them_ .

a Jane had a problem with her work, so we talked _____ over _____ , and now it's fine.

b I'm just like my mother. I take _____ after _____ in every way.

c There are problems with my computer. I'll sort _____ out _____ tomorrow.

d I used to like Ann, but since you told me what she did to you, I've really gone _____ off _____ .

e We were going to have a meeting, but we had to call _____ off _____ at the last minute.

f There are clothes all over your bedroom. Please put _____ away _____ .

g If you're going out with your baby brother, you'd better look _____ after _____ .

h I'm sorry you had a complaint about your room. I'll look _____ into _____ right away.

i My dog died last week. I don't think I'll ever get _____ over _____ .

j I need a calculator to work out how much money I've got left. I can't work _____ out _____ in my head.

k I wish you'd stop getting at me. You're always putting _____ down _____ .

Pronunciation

11 Sounds and spelling

1 **T 5.3** Put a circle around the symbol that matches the sound <u>underlined</u> in the word. All the words begin with the letter *w*.

Examples
w<u>i</u>ld   /ɪ/   (/aɪ/)   /iː/   w<u>i</u>lderness   (/ɪ/)   /aɪ/   /iː/

a w<u>o</u>n't   /ʌ/   /əʊ/   /ɒ/   w<u>a</u>nt   /æ/   /əʊ/   /ɒ/

b w<u>a</u>lk   /ɔː/   /ɑː/   /ɒ/   w<u>o</u>rk   /ɔː/   /ɜː/   /ɔɪ/

c w<u>o</u>nder   /ʌ/   /ɔː/   /ɒ/   w<u>a</u>nder   /ʌ/   /ɔː/   /ɒ/

d w<u>o</u>man   /ʊ/   /əʊ/   /ʌ/   w<u>o</u>men   /ʊ/   /əʊ/   /ɪ/

e w<u>a</u>rm   /ɔː/   /aɪ/   /ɜː/   w<u>o</u>rm   /ɔː/   /ɔɪ/   /ɜː/

f w<u>o</u>rd   /ɔː/   /ɜː/   /aɪ/   w<u>a</u>rd   /ɑː/   /aɪ/   /ɔː/

g w<u>ea</u>r   /eə/   /e/   /iː/   w<u>ea</u>ry   /eə/   /ɪə/   /iː/

h w<u>ei</u>ght   /aɪ/   /eɪ/   /e/   w<u>ei</u>rd   /aɪ/   /eɪ/   /ɪə/

2 **T 5.4** In the following groups of words, three words rhyme. <u>Underline</u> the *odd one out*.

a /ʌ/   done   <u>phone</u>   won   son
b /ʊ/   would   should   good   blood
c /uː/   move   love   prove   groove
d /əʊ/   though   through   throw   sew
e /eɪ/   weak   break   ache   shake
f /aʊ/   flower   power   tower   lower
g /ɜː/   worth   birth   north   earth
h /eɪ/   hate   wait   weight   height
i /ɪə/   fear   near   pear   clear
j /eə/   share   prayer   mayor   layer

6

Relative clauses
Participles and infinitives
Nouns in groups (1)

Defining and non-defining relative clauses

1 General knowledge quiz

Test your general knowledge on topics related to Britain. Tick (✓) the correct answer.

General Knowledge Quiz on Britain

1 *A Beefeater is …*

a ☐ a man who guards Buckingham Palace.
b ☐ a man who guards the Tower of London.
c ☐ someone who prepares the Queen's food.

2 *Yorkshire pudding is …*

a ☐ a batter that is baked in the oven and eaten with beef.
b ☐ a pudding that is only eaten in Yorkshire, in the north of England.
c ☐ a pudding that is eaten only on bank holidays.

3 *Whisky is a strong alcoholic drink made from malt,*

a ☐ which is only made in Scotland.
b ☐ which is Britain's biggest export.
c ☐ which is also used as a substitute for petrol.

4 *Concorde is …*

a ☐ the fastest plane that has ever flown.
b ☐ the heaviest plane that has ever flown.
c ☐ the only commercial aircraft that can go faster than sound.

5 *Ben Nevis is a mountain in Scotland,*

a ☐ which is also the highest mountain in Europe.
b ☐ which is also the highest mountain in the UK.
c ☐ which is also the highest mountain in the world.

6 *Virgin is a well-known British company,*

a ☐ whose chairman is one of the wealthiest people in the UK.
b ☐ whose staff have to be under forty years old.
c ☐ whose shareholders get free flights on *Virgin* planes.

7 *10 Downing Street is the house …*

a ☐ where the Mayor of London lives.
b ☐ where Prince Charles lives.
c ☐ where the Prime Minister lives.

8 *Agatha Christie is a well-known British author,*

a ☐ who is famous for writing romantic stories.
b ☐ who is famous for writing detective stories.
c ☐ who is famous for writing children's books.

9 *1066 is the year when …*

a ☐ the Great Plague happened.
b ☐ the Great Fire took place.
c ☐ William the Conquerer invaded Britain.

10 *Stratford-upon-Avon is a provincial English town …*

a ☐ where William Shakespeare was born.
b ☐ where King Henry VIII died.
c ☐ where you can bathe in hot, underground springs.

2 Defining or non-defining?

1 Are the following sentences more likely to be completed with a defining relative clause (D) or a non-defining relative clause (ND)? Write **D** or **ND** in the boxes.

a ☐ I'd love to meet someone _____
_____ .

b ☐ We're looking for a house _____ .

c ☐ We went to see *Romeo and Juliet* _____
_____ .

d ☐ Do you know a shop _____
_____ ?

e ☐ Marilyn Monroe _____
_____
died of an overdose of barbiturates.

f ☐ I find people _____
difficult to get on with.

g ☐ My computer _____
_____ is already out of date.

h ☐ I met a girl _____ .

i ☐ Professor James Williams _____
_____
will give a talk next week.

j ☐ I bought a ham and pickle sandwich _____
_____ .

2 **T 6.1** Here is the information missing from Exercise 1. Use it to complete the sentences. Insert a relative pronoun and commas where necessary. Leave out the relative pronoun if possible.

> You went to school with her.
> I ate it immediately.
> It has four bedrooms.
> I bought it just last year.
> They lose their temper.
> It sells second-hand furniture.
> Her real name was Norma Jean Baker.
> This person could teach me how to cook.
> It was one of the best films I've ever seen.
> Many people consider him to be the world's expert on butterflies.

3 Punctuation and omitting the pronoun

In the following sentences, insert commas if there is a non-defining relative clause. Cross out the pronoun if possible in the defining relative clauses.

> Examples
> *Sheila, who I first got to know at university, was one of six children.*
> *The man ~~who~~ you were talking to is a famous artist.*
> *This is the story that amazed the world.* (No change)

a The thing that I most regret is not going to university.

b My two daughters who are 16 and 13 are both interested in dancing.

c The town where I was born has changed dramatically.

d I didn't like the clothes which were in the sale.

e Salt that comes from the sea is considered to be the best for cooking.

f Salt whose qualities have been known since prehistoric times is used to season and preserve food.

g The CD that I bought yesterday doesn't work.

h You know the book that you paid £20 for? I just got it for £5.

i The area of England where I'd most like to live is Devon, in the West Country.

j Devon where my mother's family comes from is famous for its lovely countryside and dramatic coastline.

4 All relative pronouns

1 Match a line in **A** with a line in **B**.

	A	**B**
a	Have I told you recently	when you expect to arrive.
b	I have to do	where my brother lives.
c	I love garlic in all my food,	which greatly surprised my teachers.
d	We're emigrating to Australia,	whose hair came down to her waist.
e	I met a girl	how much I love you?
f	I passed all my exams,	whatever you want.
g	Let me know	which is why I'm always brushing my teeth.
h	Being generous, I'll buy you	what I believe to be right.

2 Fill the gaps with a relative pronoun. If the pronoun can be omitted, add nothing.

a The lady _____ is sitting in the wheelchair is my grandmother.

b I know an Italian restaurant _____ serves excellent home-made pasta.

c I know an Italian restaurant _____ you can always get a table.

d Uncle Tom earns a fortune, _____ is why I've asked him to lend me £1,000.

e Sean is a child _____ people immediately like.

f My daughter, _____ ambition is to emigrate to Australia, has finally got her visa.

g I gave him a drink of water, _____ he drank thirstily.

h The flight _____ we wanted to get was fully booked.

i My Auntie's house is the place _____ I feel most at home.

j This is the smallest car _____ has ever been made.

k That's the man _____ wife left him because he kept his pet snake in their bedroom.

l I love the things _____ you say to me.

m I go shopping at the new shopping centre, _____ there's always free parking.

n She told me she'd been married before, _____ I didn't realize.

o _____ you do, don't touch that button. The machine will explode.

5 Prepositions in relative clauses

Combine the sentences, remembering to put the preposition after the verb in the relative clause.

Example
I want you to meet the people. I work with them.
*I want you to meet the people I work **with**.*

a This is the book. I was telling you about it.

_____

b She's a friend. I can always rely on her.

_____

c That's the man. The police were looking for him.

_____

d She recommended a book by Robert Palmer. I'd never heard of him.

_____

e You paid £500 for a carpet. It has been reduced to £200.

The carpet _____

f The Prime Minister gave a good speech. I agree with his views.

_____

g He spoke about the environment. I care deeply about this.

_____

h What's that music? You're listening to it.

_____

i Her mother died last week. She looked after her for many years.

_____

j My daughter has started smoking. I disapprove of this.

_____

Participles

6 Participles as adjectives

Complete the gaps with -ed or -ing.

Examples
a shock*ing* story
a reserv*ed* seat

a   scream_____ children

b   a satisfi_____ customer

c   a disgust_____ meal

d   a confus_____ explanation

e   a cake load_____ with calories

f   a house in an expos_____ position

g   a conceit_____ person

h   a frighten_____ film

i   an exhaust_____ walk

j   disappoint_____ exam results

k   a bor_____ exercise

l   a tir_____ journey

m   an unexpect_____ surprise

n   disturb_____ news

o   a thrill_____ story

p   a relax_____ holiday

q   a block_____ nose

r   a disappoint_____ customer

s   well-behav_____ children

t   a promis_____ start

7 Participle clauses

1   Rewrite the sentences to include a participle clause instead of a relative clause.

Example
Can you see the woman who's dressed in red and sitting in the corner?
Can you see the woman dressed in red sitting in the corner?

a   People who live in blocks of flats often complain of loneliness.

_____

_____

b   Letters that are posted before 5 p.m. should arrive the next day.

_____

_____

c   The train that is standing on platform 5 is for Manchester.

_____

_____

d   Firemen have rescued passengers who were trapped in the accident.

_____

_____

e   It took workmen days to clear up the litter that was dropped by the crowds.

_____

_____

f   They live in a lovely house that overlooks the River Thames.

_____

_____

2   Fill the gaps with a verb from the box in either its present or past participle form.

Example
Jo was in a bad mood for the whole week, completely *ruining* our holiday.

feel	borrow	explain	say	direct
study	finish	take	know	steal

a   After _____ her exams, Maggie went out to celebrate.

b   Jewellery _____ in the robbery has never been recovered.

c   I got a letter from the Tax Office _____ that I owe them £1,000.

d   _____ hungry, I decided to make myself a sandwich.

e   Books _____ from the library must be returned in two weeks.

f   Not _____ what to do, she burst out crying.

g   I had a long talk with Jack, _____ why it was important for him to work hard.

h   _____ everything into consideration, I've decided to give you a second chance.

i   *Birdman*, _____ by Stephen Spielberg, will be released next month.

j   With both children _____ at university, the house seems really quiet.

Infinitive clauses

8 I didn't know what to do

It's Julia's 21st birthday party, and she has a lot of problems! Complete the sentences with a question word and an infinitive.

Example
Shall I wear my red skirt or my blue one?
She doesn't know _which skirt to wear_.

a 'Shall I invite people for 7.00? Or 8.00? Or 9.00?'

She can't decide _____

_____ .

b 'Should I invite Suzie or not?'

She isn't sure _____

_____ or not.

c 'I could invite people by e-mail if I knew how to use it.'

She wants someone to show her

_____ .

d 'Shall I buy beer? Wine? Sherry? Cider?'

She can't decide _____

_____ .

e 'Shall I invite ten people? Thirty people? Fifty people?'

She doesn't know _____

_____ .

Revision of relatives, participles, and infinitives

9 Boy breaks into MI5 computer system

T 6.2 Read the text about Max. There are gaps in the text. Fill the gaps with a clause from the box. Write a number **1–14**.

Max White is only ten years old, but he has the honour of being the youngest person (a) [ ] . Max, (b) [ ] , created havoc with MI5's computer system and nearly caused a national emergency. Max just thought he was having fun (c) [ ] .

Max was just six years old when his father bought him his first computer, (d) [ ] , but he quickly moved on to more exciting activities.

Max, (e) [ ] , had soon infiltrated all his father's confidential files. Max was too young to understand the seriousness of (f) [ ] .

Early in the morning he would creep into his father's office, (g) [ ] , and turn on the computer. He realized that different codes gave him access to certain files, and he soon discovered files (h) [ ] .

Keith Hamilton, (i) [ ] , monitored the progress of this unknown spy. He wondered what sort of super intelligence could break the codes (j) [ ] . But what he couldn't understand was why the spy made no attempt to close all the files behind him, thus (k) [ ] that espionage was taking place.

The reason became apparent when they discovered their so-called secret agent. Max didn't know (l) [ ] the files, only how to open them. This incident has been an expensive lesson for MI5, (m) [ ] .

Max doesn't really understand (n) [ ] , but he has promised to stick to Super Mario and Nintendo from now on.

1 whose father is the Chief Inspector of the Metropolitan Police

2 what he was doing

3 which they thought were indecipherable

4 that even his father was unaware of

5 making it obvious

6 how to close down

7 playing a computer game

8 why everyone is making such a fuss

9 which he used to play children's games on

10 that has ever fooled the Security Services of MI5

11 who is the Government Section Chief of MI5

12 who have had to change their whole computer system

13 who is eleven next month

14 closing the door gently behind him

Nouns in groups (1)

10 *a three-mile walk*

> Look at these examples of number + noun + noun.
>   *a three-mile walk*
>   *a sixteen-year-old girl*
>   *a ten-hour flight*
> These are expressions of measurement before a noun. Note that the number and the first noun are joined with a hyphen, and that the first noun is usually in the singular.

Put the information before the noun.

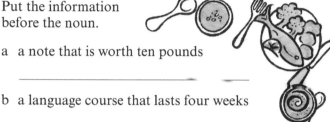

a   a note that is worth ten pounds

_____

b   a language course that lasts four weeks

_____

c   a drive that takes three hours

_____

d   a meal that consists of three courses

_____

e   a holiday that lasts two weeks

_____

f   a delay at the airport that went on or two hours

_____

g   a letter that goes on for ten pages

_____

h   a university course that takes three years

_____

i   a prison sentence of ten years

_____

j   a hotel with five stars

_____

k   a speed limit of 30 miles an hour

_____

l   a house that was built two hundred years ago

_____

Vocabulary

11 People, places, and things

Here are eighteen adjectives. Divide them into three groups – describing people, describing places, and describing things. There are six in each group.

obstinate	breathtaking	cunning	spoilt
unspoilt	aggressive	picturesque	automatic
hand-made	deserted	arrogant	accurate
waterproof	overgrown	long-lasting	artificial
easy-going	overcrowded		

People	Places	Things

12 Similar words, different meaning

Here are some pairs of adjectives that are easy to confuse. Fill the gap with the correct adjective.

   unreadable   illegible

a   I couldn't work out who the letter was from. The signature was _____ .

b   I know Shakespeare is very popular but I find him totally _____ .

   childish   childlike

c   Sarah is so _____ . She's always having temper tantrums.

d   It was wonderful to watch the tiny lambs playing, I got such _____ pleasure from the experience.

   sensible   sensitive

e   Sophie is extremely _____ at the moment. Anything you say seems to upset her.

f   Karen is not a very _____ person. She wore high-heeled shoes for our four-mile walk.

   true   truthful

g   I've never known her to tell a lie. She's a very _____ person.

h   I can never watch sad films that are based on a _____ story. They always make me cry.

intolerable   intolerant

i   Susan is so _____ of other people. She never accepts anyone else's opinion, and she always thinks she knows best.

j   I find Mark's behaviour _____ . It's unfair to be so selfish.

economic   economical

k   We're having an _____ crisis at the moment. James has lost his job and I don't know how we are going to pay the mortgage.

l   It's more _____ to drive slowly. You can do a lot more miles to the gallon.

Prepositions

13 Adjective + preposition

Put the correct preposition into each gap.

a   Are you afraid _____ the dark?

b   She was angry _____ me _____ not telling her the news.

c   Canterbury is famous _____ its cathedral.

d   Bill is jealous _____ me because I'm cleverer than him.

e   I'm very proud _____ my two daughters.

f   I'm disappointed _____ you. I thought I could trust you.

g   You're very different _____ your brother.

    I thought you'd be similar _____ each other.

h   Are you excited _____ going on holiday?

i   Visitors to Britain aren't used _____ driving on the left.

j   Visitors to hot countries need to be aware _____ the risk of malaria.

k   You should be ashamed _____ what you did.

l   I am most grateful _____ all your help.

m Who is responsible _____ this mess?

n   My son is crazy _____ a pop group called *Hanson*.

o   What's wrong _____ you? You don't look well.

Pronunciation

14 Silent consonants

1   T 6.3   English words often have silent consonants.

    Examples
    k̶now   w̶riter   wal̶k   lamb̶

Put the words below into the correct column according to whether or not they have silent consonants. Cross out the silent letters.
Use your dictionary to check pronunciation.

b̶omb̶	listen	i̶ndustry̶	computer
gadget	honest	continent	receipt
recipe	mortgage	fasten	eccentric
insect	lamp	hooligan	heirloom
whistle	stadium	straight	forest
citizen	fascinating	sandwich	exhausted

A all consonants pronounced	B some consonants not pronounced
industry	bomb̶

2   T 6.4   Transcribe these words from phonetics. They all have silent letters.

a   /saɪənˈtɪfɪk/   _____

b   /saɪˈkɒlədʒɪst/   _____

c   /ˈhænsəm/   _____

d   /rɪˈsɜːtʃ/   _____

e   /ˈkrɪsməs/   _____

f   /ˈfrenʃɪp/   _____

g   /klaɪm/   _____

h   /ˈgrænfɑːðə/   _____

i   /kæmˈpeɪn/   _____

j   /ˈwenzdeɪ/   _____

k   /kɑːm/   _____

l   /ˈwɪskɪ/   _____

Verb patterns

1 Basic verb patterns

Match a line in **A** with a line in **B**.

A	B
a I enjoy	waiting in queues. It really annoys me.
b I look forward	to buy anything. I'm broke.
c You need	to do tonight?
d I finished	doing tonight?
e My dad promised	to see you again soon.
f I hope	to seeing you again soon.
g Anna chose	do the washing-up.
h What do you feel like	to wear her black suede skirt for the party.
i I can't afford	cooking. I find it very creative.
j I can't stand	painting the bathroom last night.
k Beth helped me	to buy me a stereo if I passed my exams.
l What would you like	to book if you want to eat at *Guido's*.

2 Using a dictionary

1 Look at the dictionary extract. It shows which verb patterns are possible. Some of the verb patterns in the sentences are right, and some are wrong. Tick (✓) those that are right, and correct those that are wrong.

> **stop** /stɒp/ *v* (**-pp-**) **1** to put an end to the movement, progress, operation, etc of a person or thing: *stop a taxi* ◦ *Can you stop the machine?* ◦ *I had to stop somebody in the street to ask the way.* **2** to end or finish an activity: *stop work* ◦ *He never stops talking.* ◦ *She's stopped smoking.* ◦ *Has it stopped raining yet?* **3** ~ **sb/sth** (**from**) **doing sth** to prevent sb from doing sth or sth from happening: *I'm sure he'll go, there's nothing to stop him.* ◦ *You can't stop our going/us (from) going if we want to.* ◦ *We bandaged his wound but couldn't stop it bleeding.* **4** (**a**) to finish moving, happening or operating: ◦ *Does this train stop at Oxford?* (**b**) to end an activity temporarily; to pause: *We stopped for a while to admire the scenery.* ◦ *She never stopped to consider that others might object.*

a ☐ They were completely lost so they stopped asking for directions.

b ☐ I stopped working when I had a baby.

c ☐ I stopped play tennis when I twisted my ankle.

d ☐ The rain was so heavy that there was nothing we could do to stop the kitchen against flooding.

e ☐ The policeman stopped me from asking why I was driving at over 100 miles an hour.

f ☐ We went home when the sun stopped to shine.

g ☐ You can't stop me telling everyone what I know about you.

h ☐ He couldn't stop his son from go to the all-night party.

2 Use your dictionary to decide if the *-ing* form or infinitive is used correctly in these sentences. If there is a mistake, correct it.

Example

    ✗ They denied ~~to steal~~ *stealing* the money.

a ☐ I seem to have lost my passport.

b ☐ I avoid to travel in the rush-hour if I can.

c ☐ Have you considered to work abroad?

d ☐ We expected him arriving yesterday.

e ☐ We agreed to meet outside the cinema.

f ☐ I've arranged collecting Kate from school at four o'clock.

g ☐ Karen decided not to go to the party. She was too tired.

h ☐ I can't help to love him, even though he is selfish and inconsiderate.

i ☐ I offered give David a lift but he said he'd rather walk.

j ☐ I can't get used to seeing my daughter driving a car.

k ☐ He admitted attempting to smuggle diamonds into the country.

l ☐ I suggest to go to a restaurant tonight.

m ☐ I want that you come home early.

3 More complex verb patterns

1 Make sentences from the words in the columns.
The sentences must make sense!

My brother wants	me	to be late.
Our hosts would hate	you	to do well in my exams.
My aunt would love		do the exercise again.
The doctor warned	us	do what we wanted.
My parents expect	my son	to fix his bike.
The guide advised	our friends	to take over my business.
The policeman told	the tourists	to stay close.
We invited all	the driver	to come to a party.
The teacher made		to slow down.
My grandparents let	her class	not to work so hard.
I'd like	his patient	to visit her more often.

2 Rewrite the sentences so that they have a similar meaning. Use the prompts. Include an infinitive or an *-ing* form.

Example
I couldn't go to the party last night. (allowed)
I wasn't allowed to go to the party last night.

a I was surprised to see Ben at the party. (expect)

_____

b We're having dinner at the Greens' on Saturday. (invited)

_____

_____

c I should have a hair-cut. (need)

_____

d I can't wait to see you in June. (looking forward)

_____

e What shall I have for dessert? (can't decide)

_____

f The teacher said we could go home early. (let)

_____

g But she said we had to do extra homework. (made)

_____

h Can you wait for a minute? (mind)

_____

i I'd prefer to have tea. (rather)

_____

j Let's wait before we make a decision. (suggest)

_____

_____

k 'I'll lend you some money,' she said to me. (offered)

_____

l 'Please don't make a noise,' he said to me. (asked)

_____

m 'I'm sorry I woke you up,' I said to my neighbours. (apologized)

_____

_____

4 -ing or infinitive?

Put the verb in brackets in either the -ing form or the infinitive.

a I used _____ (think) that life ended at 40, but now I'm 41 I know it's not true.

It's five in the morning. I'm not used to _____ (get) up this early.

b Remember _____ (lock) the door when you leave the house.

I remember _____ (fall) out of my pram when I was a baby.

c Stop _____ (make) such a terrible noise.

Carol stopped _____ (make) herself a cup of tea.

d I mustn't forget _____ (buy) Jane a birthday card.

I'll never forget _____ (meet) my husband for the first time.

e I've always tried _____ (do) my best.

If you can't do this exercise, try _____ (ask) a friend for help.

f I started _____ (play) golf last year.

Oh, look! It's starting _____ (rain).

g I need _____ (speak) to you.

The house needs _____ (paint).

h Do you like _____ (cook)?

I like _____ (cook) something special when guests come.

I like _____ (pay) bills on time.

Verb patterns with other parts of speech

5 Adjectives, nouns, and prepositions

1 Fill the gaps with one of the adjectives from the box.

sorry	delighted	safe	mean
kind	nice	interesting	impossible

a It's _____ to cut with this knife. It's blunt.

b It was very _____ to meet you. Goodbye.

c Is it _____ to walk here alone at night?

d It was very _____ of John to buy such a cheap present.

e We were all _____ to hear your good news.

f It was very _____ of you to give me a lift.

g I'm _____ to hear that your mother isn't well.

h She's very _____ to talk to. We had some good chats.

2 Fill the gaps with a noun and an infinitive.

anyone	things	to visit	to pay
nothing	way	to do	to go
money	time	to shout	to talk
need	idea	to wear	to skin

a It's _____ _____ . Hurry up, or we'll be late.

b The chef showed me the correct _____ _____ a fish.

c It's a good _____ _____ the dentist twice a year.

d I'm lonely. I haven't got _____ _____ to.

e There's no _____ _____ . I can hear you just fine.

f I have so many _____ _____ . I don't know where to start.

g Have you got enough _____ _____ for the tickets?

h My clothes are all old. I have _____ _____ for the party.

3 Fill the gaps with a preposition and an *-ing* form.

about	like
without	by
with	of
at	for

having	remembering	doing
making	being stung	coming
buying	arriving	
asking	going	

a I got into trouble _____ _____ at school late.

b You can lose weight _____ _____ exercise.

c How _____ _____ out for a meal tonight?

d How dare you take my money _____ _____ me?

e I'm fed up _____ _____ no money.

f This machine is used _____ _____ pasta.

g I'm hopeless _____ _____ people's names.

h I'm thinking _____ _____ a new car. A Renault, maybe.

i Thank you _____ _____ to see me.

j Yuk! Monday morning! I don't feel _____ _____ to work!

k I'm always afraid _____ _____ by a wasp.

Infinitives

6 Forms of the infinitive

Write in the correct form of the infinitive of the verb in brackets.

Examples
This tree should *be chopped* (chop) down. It's dangerous.
We agreed *to meet* (meet) each other outside the cinema.
It's great *to have finished* (finish) our exams.

a She's late. She must _____ (forget) our appointment.

b He hopes _____ (select) to play in next week's football match.

c I offered _____ (pay) for the meal, but she refused.

d I'd like _____ (meet) Princess Diana.

e I sent my suit _____ (dry-clean).

f Sue and Richard are always arguing. They seem _____ (have) a few problems.

g I'm sorry _____ (disturb) you, but can you tell me the time?

h You should _____ (work), not watching the television.

i I'd like _____ (see) her face when you told her the news!

j I'm glad I'm not famous. I'd hate _____ (recognize) all the time.

k You should _____ (tell) me you were coming.

l This homework is late. It was meant _____ (hand) in last week.

7 I don't want to

T 7.1 Match a line (a–j) with a line (1–10).

a ☐ We'd love to have a holiday,

b ☐ Why don't you come to our house?

c ☐ Make sure you're back early tonight.

d ☐ I don't smoke any more, but

e ☐ Mum, have you mended my jeans?

f ☐ Have you asked Jill to go out with you?

g ☐ You've broken my antique vase!

h ☐ Why are you going away?

i ☐ Can you chew gum at school?

j ☐ Did you get to the end of the exam?

1 I'm sorry. I haven't had time to.

2 I used to.

3 Because I have to. It's a business trip.

4 I'm sorry. I didn't mean to.

5 No, we aren't allowed to.

6 I'll try to, but it depends on the traffic.

7 but we can't afford to.

8 Yes, I just managed to.

9 I'd love to. Thank you!

10 No. I want to, but I'm too shy.

Revision of infinitives and *-ing* forms

8 The house that Jack built

Put the correct verb into each gap.
Use either the infinitive or the *-ing* form.

pay	repay	listen	leave	celebrate	build	be
live	make	do (×2)	give	work (×2)	lend	

Jack Baines is a self-made millionaire, but his beginnings were very lowly. He was the youngest of eight children. His father had a job in the cotton mills of Blackburn, Lancashire in the 1920s, but he was often unable (**a**) _____ due to poor health. The family couldn't afford (**b**) _____ the rent or bills, and the children often went hungry. After (**c**) _____ school at the age of 14, Jack was wondering what (**d**) _____ when Mr Walker, his old teacher, offered (**e**) _____ him £100 to start his own business.

It was just after the war. Raw materials were scarce, and Jack (without (**f**) _____ to his parents' advice) saw a future in scrap metal. He bought bits of metal and stored them in an old garage. When he had built up a sizeable amount, he sold it to local industries for a vast profit.

Jack enjoyed (**g**) _____ hard and was encouraged (**h**) _____ the most of his potential by Mr Walker. After one year he had succeeded in (**i**) _____ the £100 loan and he also managed (**j**) _____ Mr Walker £100 interest to thank him for his generosity.

By the time Jack was 30 years old he had made his first million, and he wanted (**k**) _____ this achievement by (**l**) _____ something 'grand'. With all his money it was now possible (**m**) _____ a beautiful home for himself and his parents . In 1959 'Baines Castle' was built in the heart of the Lancashire countryside. It was one of the finest buildings in the county.

Jack has recently sold 'Baines Steel' for a staggering £500 million, but Jack still can't get used to (**n**) _____ the good life. He can often be found at the local pub drinking pints with the locals.

'I remember (**o**) _____ very poor as a child but never unhappy,' says Jack, 'and I never forget where I come from and who I am.'

Lancashire people are proud of their local hero, and if a visitor asks the origins of the 'grand' castle on the hill the locals say 'Why, it's the house that Jack built'.

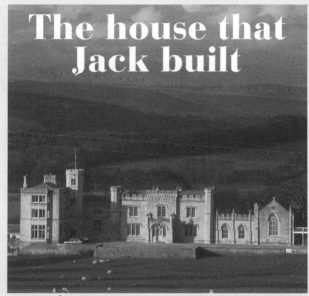

The house that Jack built

9 Verbs of perception

1 Certain verbs express perception, for example, *see*, *hear*, *watch*, *feel*, *smell*, *sense*, *observe*, *notice*, *spot*. They can be used with both the infinitive (without *to*) and the *-ing* form.

> I could **hear** her **crying** all night long.
> I didn't **hear** you **come** in last night.

2 The use of the *-ing* form suggests the activity has duration. It is in progress at the time it is perceived, and it continues afterwards.

> We **heard** him **playing** the piano.
> I can **smell** something **burning**.

3 The use of the infinitive suggests the whole, completed action is perceived.

> I **saw** the girl **fall** off her horse.
> I **saw** her **walk** across the room and **take** a gun out of the desk drawer.

Complete the sentences with either the infinitive without *to* or the *-ing* form of the verb in brackets.

a When I woke up, I could hear the birds _____ (sing).

b But then I heard my brother _____ (slam) the bathroom door.

c Soon I could smell bacon _____ (cook).

d From our hotel window we could see people _____ (play) and _____ (sunbathe) on the beach.

e I saw her _____ (pick) up the letter from the mat and _____ (rip) open the envelope.

f When I got to the cinema, I spotted my friend _____ (wait) for me.

g Over the years I watched the new airport _____ (build).

h I knew the guests had arrived because I could hear them _____ (laugh) downstairs.

i I've never seen anyone _____ (eat) as much as you do.

j I noticed a girl _____ (shoplift). I saw her _____ (take) a bottle of perfume from a shelf and _____ (put) it in her bag.

10 Compound nouns

Put one word in each box to form three compound nouns. Remember that some compound nouns are written as one word, some as two words, and some are hyphenated. Check the spelling in your dictionary.

a | [   ] test / pressure / donor

b | camp / building / bomb [   ]

c | [   ] fall / melon / skiing

d | [   ] house / grocer / salad

e | [   ] club / mare / shift

f | brief / suit / book [   ]

g | paper / plastic / shoulder [   ]

h | [   ] bow / coat / drop

i | [   ] shine / rise / set

j | [   ] works / sign / rage

k | black / floor / notice [   ]

l | [   ] light / break / dream

m | [   ] shake / writing / book

n | [   ] cube / berg / rink

o | [   ] cake / present / card

p | [   ] scape / lady / slide

q | [   ] car / centre / ground

r | address / visitors' / note [   ]

Phrasal verbs

11 Type 4

> 1 Type 4 phrasal verbs consist of a verb + an adverb +
>   a preposition. The preposition has an object.
>   *Do you **get on with** your neighbours?*
>   *We've **run out of** sugar.*
>
> 2 The word order cannot change.
>   *Do you **get on with them**?*
>   **Do you get on them with?*
>   *We've **run out of it**.*
>   **We've run out it of.*
>
> 3 Dictionaries show type 4 phrasal verbs by giving
>   both the adverb and the preposition.
>   **get away with sth**
>
> 4 Sometimes a phrasal verb can be type 4 or type 1.
>   Dictionaries show this.
>   **break up (with sb)**
>   *They **broke up** after five years' marriage.*
>   *She's sad because she's just **broken up with**
>   her boyfriend.*

Complete the sentences using one of the combinations
in the box.

| up with | up to | in with | away with (×2) | away from |
| on with | up for | out with | down on (×2) | up against |

a Keep _____ me! I've got a terrible cold,
  and I don't want you to catch it.

b We must try to cut _____ the amount of
  money we spend a month. We spend more than we
  earn.

c Don't let me disturb you. Carry _____
  your work.

d Face _____ reality. You've got to realize
  that you are responsible for your own actions.

e She's such a snob. She looks _____
  everyone who doesn't have as much money as she
  does.

f His crime was really quite serious, so he was lucky

  to get _____ a fine rather than a prison
  sentence.

g I know you're disappointed that we didn't have a
  summer holiday this year. We'll try to get a few days

  away in the autumn to make _____ it.

h There is a move in Britain to do _____
  the monarchy completely, so that Britain would
  become a republic.

i My daughter had a few weeks off school recently.
  When she went back, she had to try hard to catch

  _____ all the work she had missed.

j Jane's a very argumentative person. She's always

  having rows with people and falling _____
  them.

k The government has come _____ a big
  problem in their economic policy. The unions won't
  co-operate, and management doesn't approve of
  what they're trying to do.

l The antique table is very nice, but it doesn't fit

  _____ the rest of the furniture, which is
  modern.

Pronunciation

12 Weak and strong forms

> **T 7.2** Auxiliary verbs have weak and strong forms, depending on whether they are stressed or unstressed.
>
> 1 Sometimes the weak form is a contraction.
>
>   he is   = he's
>   she does not = she doesn't
>   I have not   = I haven't
>
> 2 Sometimes the weak form is a change in the vowel sound. This is often a change to /ə/.
>
> | | Weak | Strong |
> |---|---|---|
> | was | /wəz/ | /wɒz/ |
> | | Was Tom there? | Yes, he was. |
> | were | /wə/ | /wɜː/ |
> | | Were you there? | Yes, we were. |
> | can | /kən/ | /kæn/ (can't = /kɑːnt/) |
> | | Can you swim? | Yes, I can. |
> | been | /bɪn/ | /biːn/ |
> | | I've been shopping. | Where have you been? |
>
> Some prepositions also have weak and strong vowel sounds.
>
> | | Weak | Strong | | Weak | Strong |
> |---|---|---|---|---|---|
> | to | /tə/ | /tuː/ | for | /fə/ | /fɔː/ |
> | of | /əv/ | /ɒv/ | from | /frəm/ | /frɒm/ |
> | at | /ət/ | /æt/ | | | |

1 **T 7.3** These sentences sound very unnatural. Rewrite them in more natural English with contractions where appropriate. Underline like this ·········· all auxiliaries and prepositions with weak vowel sounds.
Underline like this _____ all those with strong vowels.

Example
I do not want to see him, but I am sure you want to.
I don't want to see him but I'm sure you want to.

a She is not going to learn from this experience, but he is.

b I have heard that you are thinking of moving from London. Are you?

c They have dinner at seven, do not they?

d You will be able to get a ticket for me, will you not?

e I have got no idea who this letter is from.

f Can you not remember who Bill used to work for?

g I have been waiting for you to come. Where were you?

h We had been looking forward to coming for ages, then at the last minute we were not able to.

i Will you not sit down for a couple of minutes?

2 **T 7.4** Transcribe **A**'s lines in the following telephone conversation between two friends. Punctuate the lines carefully to make the meaning clear.

A /wɒt ə juː duːɪŋ ət ðə wiːkend/ ?

_____

B I haven't decided yet.

A /wɪə gəʊɪŋ tə skɒtlənd djʊ wɒnə kʌm tuː/ ?

_____

_____

B I'd love to. Where are you staying?

A /wiv dɪsɑɪðəd tə kæmp nʌn əv ʌs kən əfɔːd tə peɪ fərə həʊtel/

_____

_____

B Camping in Scotland in October! You'll be freezing.

A /nəʊ wi wəʊnt wiv gɒt strɒŋ tents lɒts əv wɔːm kləʊz ən θɪk sliːpɪŋ bægz/

_____

B Have you checked the weather forecast?

A /əv kɔːs wi hæv ənd ɪts prɪti wɔːm fər ɒktəʊbə/

_____

B OK then. It'll be quite an adventure!

A /eksələnt aɪl tel ðɪ ʌðəz ðeɪl bi dɪlaɪtəd wɪəl pɪk juː ʌp ət sɪks ɒn fraɪdeɪ siː juː ðen gʊdbaɪ/

_____

B Bye!

8 Modal auxiliary verbs
need and *needn't have*

Modal verbs of probability

1 How certain?

T 8.1 Read the sentences and decide on the degree of certainty expressed.
Put two ticks (✔✔) if the idea expressed is certain.
Put one tick (✔) if it is a possibility.

Examples
✔✔ I'll see you tomorrow at ten o'clock.
✔ Take your umbrella. It might rain.

a ☐ Don't worry. Everything will be all right.
b ☐ We might be moving to Oxford.
c ☐ That must be John's new car.
d ☐ He can't have been telling the truth.
e ☐ He might have left a message on the answering machine.
f ☐ Jane will be arriving any time now.
g ☐ I don't know where she is. She may have gone shopping.
h ☐ They haven't arrived yet. They can't be coming.
i ☐ 'Where's Ann?' 'She could be washing her hair.'
j ☐ She must have been very upset when you told her the news.
k ☐ You ought to pass the exam. You've done a lot of revision.
l ☐ It shouldn't be difficult to find the Science Museum. It's well signposted.

2 Present probability

T 8.2 Respond to the statements or questions using the words in brackets. Put the verb in its correct form.

Examples
Jane's got lots of spots. (might, chicken pox)
She might have chicken pox.

Harry is packing his suitcase. (must, go on holiday)
He must be going on holiday.

a Jenny looks really unhappy. (must, miss, boyfriend)

_____

b Who's at the front door? (will, Tom)

_____

c Where's Kate? It's eleven o'clock in the morning! (can't, still, sleep)

_____

d Where are the scissors? (should, the top drawer)

_____

e Why are all the lights on in their house? (could, have, party)

_____

f James has been working all night. (must, deadline to meet)

_____

g It's been snowing all night. (might, difficult, drive, work)

_____

h Timmy can't find his little sister. (may, hide, in the wardrobe)

_____

3 Past probability

1   Use the table to give an explanation
for each of the situations below.

He She They	must have can't have might have should have	cut it gone mislaid arrived home got engaged had been doing been making	a cake. a party last night. to Andy. something naughty. for ages. without me. by now. my number.

a   Stella's wearing a beautiful diamond ring.

_____

b   Look at the length of the grass in Bill's garden.

_____

c   The children ran away laughing and giggling.

_____

d   There's flour on grandma's nose.

_____

e   Paul and Gary said they'd wait for me, but I can't see them.

_____

f   Clive's flat is so clean and tidy.

_____

g   It's after midnight. Henry and Sally left ages ago.

_____

h   I don't know why Tara didn't ring.

_____

2   Do the same with this table. Note that here the perfect infinitive passive is used.

It They	must have been can't have been	watered given washed shattered blown down mended	by the wind. by a stone. properly. for a long time. enough to eat. with something red.

a   A tree has fallen across the road.

_____

b   My white jeans have turned pink!

_____

c   My TV has broken and I've only just had it fixed.

_____

d   David's pet goldfish has died.

_____

e   All the flowers in the garden have died.

_____

f   The car windscreen is broken.

_____

3   Make sentences from the table.

If I go to India I If I went to India I If I'd gone to India I	can will may might would could	see the Taj Mahal. have seen the Taj Mahal.

_____

_____

_____

_____

_____

_____

_____

_____

4 Deductions about the present and past

T 8.3   Complete the sentences, putting the verbs in brackets into the correct form.

a 'What are all those people doing with those lights and cameras?'

'They _____ (must/make) a film.'

b 'I wonder how the thief got into our apartment?'

'He _____ (could/use) the fire escape or he _____ (might/climb up) that tree.'

c 'I saw Harry waving someone off in a taxi.'

'That _____ (would/be) his cousin from Australia.'

d 'Bill told me that he'd spent £50,000 on a birthday present for his girlfriend, but he _____ _____ (may/joke). He _____ (can't/spend) that much.'

'I think you _____ (must/mishear) him.'

e 'It's five past eleven. Ken and Cathy's plane _____ _____ (should/touch down) in Kennedy Airport right now.'

'Your watch _____ (must/be) slow. It's nearly half past. Their plane _____ already _____ (will/land).'

f 'Bring very warm clothes. It _____ (could/snow) when we arrive. It _____ (can/snow) in the mountains even in summer.'

Revision of all modals

5 Meaning check

Each modal auxiliary verb has several different meanings. For each of the following sentences, two explanations are given. Tick the most likely explanation.

Example

Megan *should* get good results in her exams.

☒ Megan has an *obligation* to get good results in her exams.

☑ It is *probable* Megan will get good results in her exams.

a **I *couldn't* swim until I was 16 years old.**

☐ I didn't have *permission* to swim until I was 16 years old.

☐ I didn't have the *ability* to swim until I was 16 years old.

b **Passengers *may* smoke once the plane is airborne.**

☐ There is a *possibility* that passengers will smoke once the plane is airborne.

☐ Passengers have *permission* to smoke once the plane is airborne.

c **No one *can* smoke on the London Underground.**

☐ No one has the *ability* to smoke on the London Underground.

☐ No one has *permission* to smoke on the London Underground.

d **You *should* wear glasses.**

☐ My *advice* is that you wear glasses.

☐ There is a *probability* that you will have to wear glasses.

e **Will you answer the door?**

☐ Are you at some time in the *future* going to answer the door?

☐ I'm *asking* you to answer the door.

f **I *couldn't* get the top off the bottle.**

☐ I did not have *permission* to get the top off the bottle.

☐ I did not *manage* to get the top off the bottle.

g **You *must* be tired.**

☐ I am *sure* you are tired.

☐ I *order* you to be tired.

h **Andrew's got a meeting after work so he *may* not go to the party.**

☐ Andrew does not have *permission* to go to the party.

☐ There's a *possibility* Andrew won't go to the party.

i **You *needn't* have given me a lift.**

☐ You *gave* me a lift. This was very kind but *not necessary*.

☐ You *didn't give* me a lift because it *wasn't necessary*.

j **You *might* have helped to clear up after the party!**

☐ I'm angry because I think you *ought* to have helped clear up.

☐ I think that there's just a *possibility* that you helped to clear up.

6 Which modals fit?

1 Which of the words in the box will fit the sentences? Often there is more than one possibility.

will	should	can	ought to	could
must	may	have to	might	

a You _____ get your hair cut. It's much too long.

b _____ I ask you a question?

c Young children _____ be carried on this escalator.

d You _____ never get a seat on this train. It's always packed.

e I _____ be studying Mandarin Chinese next year.

f I _____ already speak five languages fluently.

g You'll _____ work much harder if you want to pass.

h It's Saturday night. There _____ be something good on TV.

i You _____ leave your valuables in the hotel safe.

j You _____ be over 1m 60 cm tall to be an air hostess.

2 <u>Underline</u> the correct answer.

a You *mustn't/shouldn't* have any problems with Jack. He's such a good baby.

b You *don't have to/mustn't* use cream in this sauce, but it makes it much tastier.

c I *couldn't/wouldn't* watch my favourite TV programme because Sue rang up for a long chat.

d Timmy's so stubborn. He just *can't/won't* do what he's told.

e I'm afraid I *cannot/may not* come to your wedding as I'm on holiday in Australia.

f I *was able to/could* get 10% off the marked price by paying in cash.

g I *should have gone/had to go* to visit Uncle Tom in hospital after work, but I was too tired.

h You *don't have to/mustn't* say a word about this to your mother. It's a surprise.

7 Obligation and permission

1 Read the article and put the correct expression from the box into the gaps.

The 1901 Teaching Contract for Female Teachers

At the beginning of the 20th century female teachers had a very restricted life. There was a set of 'golden rules' that they had to abide by or risk instant dismissal. The rules were there to make sure teachers commanded authority and respect, but for women it meant sacrificing a lot of personal freedom. Nowadays it seems quite incredible that such strict rules should be enforced on female teaching staff.

1 You _____ during the term of your contract.

2 You _____ company with other women.

3 You _____ authority and respect from your pupils at all times.

4 You _____ between 8 p.m. and 6 a.m. unless attending a school function.

5 You _____ ice-cream parlours at any time.

6 You _____ in a carriage or automobile with any man unless he is your father or brother.

7 You _____ the schoolroom floor at least once daily.

8 You _____ in plain colours of grey or black and your dresses _____ no more than 1 inch above the ankles.

9 You _____ beyond the city limits without the permission of the chairman of the board of school governors.

> cannot ride
> will not marry
> will dress
> shall sweep
> may not visit
> may not travel
> must be
> must be at home
> should command
> can only keep

2 Nancy Wilson was a teacher in Valley Road School, Sunderland from 1920 to 1929. Read her comments about it and complete them with a suitable past expression from below.

| had to | didn't have to | was allowed (to) |
| couldn't | weren't allowed to | were forbidden to |

a I was the youngest of six daughters and like many middle-class girls, I _____ become a teacher. I had no choice.

I _____ earn a living any other way.

b My day started at seven o'clock in the morning, when I _____ sweep and dust the schoolroom, and we _____ leave at the end of the day until this task was repeated.

c I had two grey dresses and I wore one of them every day. It _____ be grey. Black _____ also _____, but we _____ wear anything fashionable or colourful.

d We _____ ride in automobiles with any men except our father or brothers. This was no hardship because our family had no car.

e The most ridiculous rule of all was the one about visiting ice-cream parlours. I can't imagine why we _____ go there.

f Eventually, when I was 29, I did meet and marry a young man, Jack. Then, of course, I _____ give up teaching. You _____ continue as a married woman.

8 Present to past

Rewrite the sentences to make them refer to the past.

Example
I must post the letters.
I had to post the letters.

a I have to take the pills three times a day.

_____

b They must be away on holiday.

_____

c We can't see the top of the mountain.

_____

d He can't be a millionaire.

_____

e We mustn't shout in the classroom.

_____

f He won't go to bed.

_____

g That will be John on the phone.

_____

h You should be more careful.

_____

i You don't have to do this exercise.

_____

9 Positive to negative

Rewrite the sentences to make them negative.

a You must stop here.

_____

b We must learn the whole poem.

_____

c They had to take off their shoes.

_____

d He must be speaking Swedish.

_____

e We had to wear a uniform at school.

_____

f You'll have to help me do this exercise.

_____

need

10 need and needn't have

Need can have the forms of an ordinary verb or a modal auxiliary verb.

1 It most often has the forms of an ordinary verb. It is usually followed by an infinitive with *to*.

> She **needs** to rest.
> **Does** she **need** to rest?
> She **doesn't need** to rest.

It can be used as a modal verb in the negative and question, but mainly in the negative.

> **Need** she rest now?
> She **needn't** rest yet.

2 *Need + -ing = need + passive infinitive*

> *The house needs painting.*
> = The house needs to be painted.

3 *Need* has **two** past forms. They have different meanings:

> *didn't need to*
> = it wasn't necessary, so it probably wasn't done.
>
> *needn't have*
> = it wasn't necessary, but it was done.
>
> I **didn't need to** hurry, so I didn't. I took my time.
> I **needn't have** hurried, but I did. The film started at seven, not six.

Both are opposites of *had to*.

1 In the sentences below put an **M** when *need* is used as a modal verb and a **V** when *need* is used as an ordinary verb.

a ☐ I need to go home.

b ☐ You needn't come if you don't want to.

c ☐ Ian doesn't need to pass all his exams to get a place at university.

d ☐ More money is desperately needed to protect the world's endangered species.

e ☐ We didn't need to hurry. We had plenty of time.

f ☐ Need I pay now or can I pay later?

g ☐ I needn't have got up so early. I forgot it was Saturday.

h ☐ If you have any problems, you only need to tell us and we'll try to help.

i ☐ I need to water the garden.

j ☐ You needn't have walked home, I could have given you a lift.

2 <u>Underline</u> the correct word or words. Sometimes two are correct.

Example
I *mustn't* / <u>*needn't*</u> / <u>*don't have to*</u> do this exercise but it might help.

a You *mustn't* / *needn't* / *don't have to* think I'm always this tired and irritable after work. I've just had a bad day.

b We *mustn't* / *needn't* / *don't have to* book a table, the restaurant won't be full on a Monday night.

c Do you really *must* / *need to* / *have to* go now? Can't you stay a bit longer?

d You *mustn't* / *don't need to* / *don't have to* eat all your vegetables. Just have the carrots.

e You *didn't need to wake* / *needn't have woken* me up, I'm not going to work today.

f The doctor said that I *didn't need to take* / *didn't have to take* / *needn't have taken* the tablets any longer because the rash was so much better.

g Have I *must* / *need to* / *got to* ring and confirm my room reservation?

h We *didn't need to buy* / *needn't have bought* all that champagne for the party. Only three people came!

Vocabulary

11 Words that go together

Choose the best answer, A, B, C, or D.

a He said I hadn't given him his book, but I was _____ sure I had.
   A entirely   B totally   C quite   D rather

b If you want to _____ success in life, you have to work hard.
   A achieve   B receive   C award   D earn

c He was homesick, and he _____ all his family and friends.
   A lost   B lacked   C desired   D missed

d I wanted to put my new stereo together, but I couldn't make _____ of the instructions.
   A sight   B sense   C reality   D understanding

e If I breathe in, I get a sharp _____ in my chest.
   A hurt   B wound   C ache   D pain

f The _____ of living goes up and up. It'll never go down.
   A price   B value   C cost   D expense

g Use your time sensibly. Don't _____ it.

   A spend **B** waste **C** pass **D** lose

h First you lost your job, now your car's been stolen. You've had a lot of bad _____ recently.

   A luck **B** chance **C** fortune **D** risk

i You look worried. What's on your _____?

   A brain **B** head **C** mind **D** thoughts

j If you park your car in the wrong place, you have to pay a _____ .

   A fine **B** ticket **C** caution **D** fee

k I like watching political _____ on television.

   A rows **B** debates **C** arguments **D** conversations

l This hotel really tries hard to look after its _____ .

   A clients **B** patients **C** customers **D** guests

m I got some holiday _____ from the travel agents.

   A albums **B** manuals **C** brochures **D** handbooks

n I'm _____ a small flat for the three months I'm in London.

   A hiring **B** letting **C** booking **D** renting

12 A word puzzle

All the words in this crossword are associated with the rich and famous. Complete the crossword to reveal the vertical word.

1 An annual award in the form of a small statue, presented in the USA for excellence in the cinema.

2 The first public performance of a new play, or showing of a new film.

3 Beauty, wealth, and excitement mean that many film stars have a very ___ lifestyle.

4 A person who is rich, successful, and fashionable, and who travels a lot to expensive places.

5 An organized group of a star's fans.

6 A famous person's signature.

7 A person who is well-known in fashionable society and goes to a lot of fashionable parties, etc.

8 A big, luxury apartment at the top of a building. Expensive hotels often have a series of rooms on the top floor called the ___ suite.

9 A very large, long, expensive, comfortable car, often driven by a chauffeur. More usual in America.

10 A person employed to display clothes, hats, etc. at fashion shows.

11 Someone from the highest social class, belonging to a noble family.

13 Verb + preposition

Many verbs are followed by prepositions. Put the correct preposition into each gap.

Example
I agree *with* every word you say.

a I applied _____ the job, but I didn't get it.

b What are you all laughing _____? What's the joke?

c He died _____ a heart attack.

d She's suffering badly _____ sunburn.

e Do you believe _____ magic?

f I didn't realize that Maria was married _____ George.

g He's acted _____ three major films.

h Did you succeed _____ convincing your father you were telling the truth?

i Compared _____ you I'm not very intelligent at all!

j We've complained _____ our teacher _____ the amount of homework we get.

Pronunciation

14 Consonant clusters and connected speech

1 English has many words with groups (or clusters) of consonants.

Examples
jumped   /dʒʌmpt/
stream   /stri:m/
crisps   /krɪsps/

T 8.4 Say these words aloud and then transcribe them. They all come from Unit 8 and contain groups of consonants.

a /dʌznt/ _____

b /ʃʊdnt/ _____

c /mʌsnt/ _____

d /mʌslz/ _____

e /kræʃt/ _____

f /dɪstɪŋktli/ _____

g /speʃl/ _____

h /grʌmbld/ _____

i /θrɪld/ _____

j /mɑ:vləs/ _____

k /ɪksaɪtmənt/ _____

l /sɪksθ/ _____

m /ɪmprest/ _____

n /leŋθ/ _____

o /kʌmftəbl/ _____

2 **T 8.5** In sentences words often run into each other, making more clusters of consonants. Say the sentences aloud and then transcribe them.

Example
/hi dɪdnt send mi ə pəʊskɑ:d/
He didn't send me a postcard.

a /ðə kɑ: wɪnskri:nz smæʃt/

_____

b /maɪ ʌŋklz spreɪnd ɪz æŋkl/

_____

c /ðɪs kri:m dʌznt teɪst freʃ/

_____

d /jʊ dəʊnt hævtə skri:m/

_____

e /ði:z waɪt dʒi:nz məstəv ʃrʌŋk/

_____

f /ʃi əraɪvd drest ɪn ðə leɪtəst fæʃn/

_____

g /hi dʌznt nəʊ ɪz əʊn streŋθ/

_____

h /hi kɑ:ntəv fɪkst ɪt prɒpəli/

_____

9 Questions and negatives
I don't think you're right

Negatives

1 Negative auxiliaries

Complete the sentences with a negative auxiliary from the box.

isn't	aren't	'm not	hasn't	didn't
doesn't	don't	hadn't	won't	haven't

a Jackie speaks fluent French, but I ——————.

b We wanted to leave the party, but Fred —————— .

c I've been to America, but my parents —————— .

d I thought Volvos were made in Austria, but they —————— .

e They said the weather would be nice today, but it —————— .

f I'm going to give up smoking, but my girlfriend —————— .

g My husband's really mean with money, but I —————— .

h Jo likes Indian food, but Andrew —————— .

i Bill thought I'd forgotten our wedding anniversary, but I —————— .

j The bedroom's been decorated, but the bathroom —————— .

2 *no, not, -n't,* or *none*?

Put *no, not, -n't,* or *none* into each gap.

Examples
I'll help you, but *not* tonight.
We have *no* onions left. Sorry.
None of us understood the lesson.
The teacher was*n't* very clear.

a I asked you ———— to make a mess.

b Why did ———— you do what I asked?

c How do you manage ———— to pay any taxes?

d Bring Penny to the party, but ———— Bill. He's too loud.

e There's ———— meat in this dish, so it's suitable for vegetarians.

f 'Who likes algebra?' '———— me.'

g 'Where's the nearest swimming pool?' 'There are ———— around here.'

h She has ———— idea of how to enjoy herself.

i Why have ———— you been in touch with me for so long?

j She cooked a good risotto, but ———— the way my mother does.

k 'Do you work late?' '———— if I can help it.'

l 'Where's the coffee?' 'There's ———— left.'

m ———— plants can survive totally without water.

n I've got ———— time for people who are intolerant.

o ———— of my friends smoke.

p 'Do you like classical music?' '———— usually.'

3 Making sentences mean the opposite

Rewrite the sentences to give them the opposite meaning. Make any necessary changes.

Example
She's got lots of money.
She hasn't got any money at all.
She has absolutely no money.

a All of the students passed the exam, so their teacher was pleased.

_____

_____

b Tom was a successful businessman, who achieved a lot in his life.

_____

_____

c Our house is difficult to find. Everybody always gets lost.

_____

_____

d We had a lovely time in Venice. There weren't many people there.

_____

_____

e You must exercise your ankle. Try to move it as much as possible.

_____

_____

f I must iron my shirt. I'm going out tonight.

_____

_____

g You need to come with me. I won't go on my own.

_____

h I was in a hurry, because I needed to go to the shops.

_____

_____

i You ought to have given the dog something to eat.

_____

_____

j I told you to go to work. Why are you in bed?

_____

_____

4 *I don't think you're right*

⚠️

1 Remember that in English we usually say *I don't think* + affirmative verb rather than *I think* + negative verb. Other verbs like this are *believe, suppose,* and *expect.*
    I **don't think** I know you.
    I **don't expect** we'll meet again.
    My parents **didn't believe** I'd pass my exams.

2 We can also use the verbs *seem, expect,* and *want* in the negative followed by an infinitive.
    She **doesn't seem to be** very happy.
    I **don't expect to get** the job.
    I **don't want to go** back to that restaurant.

Rewrite the sentences, using the verb in brackets in the negative.

Example
You haven't met my wife. (I think)
I don't think you've met my wife.

a You haven't got change for a fiver. (I suppose)

_____

b This machine isn't working. (The machine seems)

_____

c It wasn't going to rain. (I thought)

_____

d Their daughter won't marry a footballer. (They want)

_____

e I wasn't going to see you at this party. (I expected)

_____

f You haven't seen Robert recently. (I suppose)

_____

g I wouldn't like snails. (I think)

_____

h You don't remember me. (I expect)

_____

i She doesn't like her job. (She seems)

_____

j She didn't get grade A in all her exams. (I believe)

_____

_____

5 Buzz Aldrin, the man on the moon

T 9.1 Read the text about Buzz Aldrin, one of the first men to walk on the moon.
Write questions for the answers.

THE MAN WHO FELL TO EARTH

BUZZ ALDRIN was part of the Apollo 11 mission in 1969 when man first walked on the moon. Neil Armstrong went first, followed by Buzz. Nothing in all his training had prepared him for that moment, and he has been travelling the world ever since, reliving the experience.

He was born in New Jersey in 1930, and he graduated from West Point Military Academy. He served as a pilot in Korea and West Germany, and in 1966 he was chosen as an astronaut.

Apollo 11 was launched to the moon on July 16. Four days later they landed near the Sea of Tranquility. The mission ended on July 24, with a splashdown in the Pacific Ocean.

On coming back to earth, he became very depressed, and suffered from alcoholism. He had married for the first time when he was young, and had three children. His second marriage lasted a very short time.

Fortunately, he seems to have found happiness and stability with his third wife, Lois Driggs Cannon, who saved him from self-destruction. They now live with their three dogs in California, and have six cars 'for fun'.

He has written his autobiography and a science fiction book, called *Encounter with Tiber*, which was published in 1996.

He now travels the world, giving lecture tours and raising funds for space exploration.

a _____ ?
  In 1969.

b _____ ?
  Neil Armstrong.

c _____
  _____ ?
  Since 1969.

d _____ ?
  In New Jersey.

e *Which* _____
  _____ ?
  West Point.

f _____ ?
  In Korea and West Germany.

g _____ ?
  In 1966.

h _____ ?
  On July 16, 1969.

i _____ ?
  Eight days.

j _____ ?
  He became very depressed.

k _____ ?
  Alcoholism.

l _____
  _____ *from his first marriage*?
  Three.

m _____ ?
  Three times.

n _____ *self-destruction*?
  Lois Driggs Cannon.

o _____ ?
  With their three dogs.

p _____ ?
  Six.

q *What sort* _____ ?
  Autobiography and science fiction.

r _____ ?
  In 1996.

s _____ *these days*?
  He gives lectures and raises funds for space exploration.

6 Dialogues and question formation

T 9.2 Complete the questions in the dialogues.

a **A** _____ that mess in the living room?
   B We did. Sorry.

   A _____ doing?
   B We just had a few friends round.

   A When _____ ?
   B We'll do it right now. Promise.

b **A** I went to a party last night.

   B _____ like?
   A It was all right, I suppose.

   B _____ talk ____ ?
   A Well, I had a bit of a chat with Vicky.

   B _____ about?
   A This and that. Mainly about Sam, her boyfriend.
       Or rather, her ex-boyfriend.

   B Oh, dear. _____ wrong?
   A They had a huge row.

   B _____ ?
   A He thought she was chatting up some other bloke,
       but she wasn't.

c **A** Did you hear about Joe? He was taken to hospital
       this afternoon.

   B _____ ?
   A Because he was attacked.

   B _____ ?
   A Some youths.

   B _____ when he was attacked?
   A He was just walking home from school.

   B _____ ?
   A Well, he's not seriously hurt, thank goodness.

   B _____ to?
   A St Mary's, the one near the stadium.

   B How long _____ in hospital?
   A Just overnight.

7 Questions and prepositions

1 Complete the questions with a preposition from the box.

| in of by with to from at about for on |

a Who was that book written _____?

b Who does this dictionary belong _____?

c What are you looking _____?

d What did you spend all your money _____?

e What is your home town famous _____?

f What sort of books are you interested _____?

g What are you talking _____?

h What are you so afraid _____?

i 'You've got a postcard.' 'Oh. Who is it _____?'

j Who are you angry _____? James or me?

2 Write a short question with a preposition in reply to
   these sentences.

   Example
   I went to the cinema last night.   *Who with?*

a I'm very cross with you.

   _____?

b We're going away for the weekend.

   _____?

c I'm very worried.

   _____?

d I'm going to Australia.

   _____*for*? A week? A month?

e I bought a present today.

   _____?

f Have you heard? Jane has got engaged.

   _____?

g Can you cut this thread for me.

   _____? I haven't got any scissors.

8 How ... ? and What ... like?

T 9.3 Write questions with either *How ...?* or *What ... like?*

Examples
How are you? I'm fine, thanks.
Sue's got a new boyfriend. *What's he like?*

a We had a new teacher today, called Peter Briscall.

_____?

b _____ today? (school)
Same as ever. Boring.

c We went to that new Thai restaurant last night.

_____? (food)

d Nice to see you. Come on in. _____? (journey)
Not too bad. Just a few hold-ups.

e Hi, Mum. I'm phoning you from Australia!

Hello, dear. _____? (weather)
It's very hot.

f I went to see my Grandma in hospital yesterday.

_____?

Not too bad.

g You should see my new flat!

_____?

h _____ these days? (your job)
OK. It could be worse.

9 Negative questions
Match a question in **A** with a line in **B**.

	A		B
a	Are you ready yet?	1	What have you been doing all this time?
b	Aren't you ready yet?	2	It's time to go.
c	Don't you want me to help you?	3	I thought you did.
d	Do you want me to help you?	4	I will if you want.
e	Aren't you a member of the tennis club?	5	I'm sure I've seen you there.
f	Are you a member of the tennis club?	6	If you are, we could have a game.
g	Don't you know the answer?	7	Yes or no?
h	Do you know the answer?	8	I'm surprised at you!
i	Don't you think it's beautiful?	9	Surely you agree with me!
j	Do you think it's beautiful?	10	I'm asking because I'm not sure.
k	Didn't I tell you I'm going out tonight?	11	I can't remember now.
l	Did I tell you I'm going out tonight?	12	I thought I had. Sorry.

Vocabulary

10 Antonyms and synonyms

1 For each of the adjectives or verbs in **A**, write its opposite in **B** using a prefix.

A	B	C
kind	*unkind*	*cruel*
honest		
credible		
appear		
fair (= equal)		
pleased		
continue		
fasten		
normal		
employed		
friendly		
trust		
professional		
known		
cover		
safe		
use		
probable		
important		
emotional		

2 In column **C**, write a synonym for the words in **B**, choosing one of the words in the box.

exceptional	reserved	damage	vanish	trivial
unbelievable	annoyed	biased	reveal	halt
hazardous	redundant	unlikely	~~cruel~~	undo
anonymous	amateur	deceitful	suspect	hostile

11 Hot Verbs *keep* and *lose*

1 Which words and expressions go with *keep*, and which go with *lose*? Tick the correct column.

keep		lose
✔	calm	
	weight	✔
	a promise	
	your way	
	going	
	in touch with sb	
	sb company	
	your nerve	
	a secret	
	sb waiting	
	your temper	
	fit	

2 Complete the sentences with one of the expressions above in the correct form.

a When you go away, please write. I'd like to —————— with you.

b When the children broke the TV, I ————— my —————— and started shouting at them.

c 'I'm tired. Can't we have a rest?' 'No. We can't stop. We must —————— until we get to the top of the mountain.'

d Can you —————— ? Jane and I have decided to get married, but don't tell anyone.

e I was going to do a bungee jump, but when I stood at the top I couldn't do it. I —————— and I had to climb down.

f I go to the gym every day because I like to —————— .

g 'Oh no! I've lost my purse!' 'Now don't panic. —————— ! When did you last have it?'

h Sorry I'm late. I took the wrong road and I ————— my —————— . I ended up miles away and I had to ask for directions.

Phrasal verbs

12 Phrasal verbs and nouns that go together

1 Some phrasal verbs have a strong association with certain objects.

Examples
set out on a journey
work out the solution to a problem
blow out the candles on a birthday cake

Match a verb in **A** with an object in **B**. Careful! There may be several possibilities, but there is usually one answer that is best.

A	B
come up with	a cupboard and throw out what you don't want
beat up	a naughty child
break into	an old man, a victim of a crime
break off	a problem, a complaint, a difficult customer
bring out	the other people in the group
bring up	a university course after one year
clear out	someone you respect
count on	a new idea, a plan
deal with	your best friend to help you
drop out of	children to be honest and hard-working
fit in with	a house, a flat, to steal something
look up to	a fact that someone might not be aware of
point out	what I said – I didn't mean it
take back	a relationship, an engagement
tell off	a new product on the market

2 Complete the sentences with one of the phrasal verbs in its correct form.

a It's time to ——————— my garage. There's so much rubbish in it that I need to get rid of.

b Waterhouse Publishers are ——————— a new book on the history of the twentieth century. It should be in the shops next month.

c The thieves ——————— the warehouse and stole goods worth £2,000.

d As they were leaving, they were disturbed by the security guard. They ——————— him ——————— and left him bleeding on the ground.

e He ——————— his elder sister, because to him she always seemed so wise and experienced.

f I accused you of being mean the other day. I ——————— it all ———————. I'm so sorry. I didn't mean it.

g 'Which one's Adam?' 'When I see him, I ——————— him ——————— to you.'

h Scientists will have to ——————— new methods of increasing the world's food supply.

i She ——————— Tom ——————— because he hit his baby sister and made her cry.

j Waiter to another waiter: 'I'll ——————— this order that has gone wrong, if you look after the customers who have just come in.'

k I had a new student in my class today. He seems very nice. I'm sure he'll ——————— the rest of the class just fine.

l Why did you ——————— university after just one term? What are you going to do with the rest of your life?

m I'm standing in the elections to be President. I hope I can ——————— your support.

n My parents ——————— me ——————— to be a Catholic, but I don't go to church any more.

Pronunciation

13 Intonation in question tags

T 9.4 In question tags the intonation either falls ▼ or rises ▲.

1 ▼ Falling intonation means that the sentence is more like a statement = 'I'm sure I'm right. Can you just confirm this for me?'

It's really warm again today, isn't it?
You've lost the car keys again, haven't you?

2 ▲ Rising intonation means that the sentence is more like a real question = 'I'm not sure if I'm right about this. Correct me if I'm wrong.'

You've been invited to Jane's party, haven't you?
John didn't fail his driving test again, did he?

Both patterns are very common in spoken English because they invite other people to join in the conversation.

1 **T 9.5** Write in the question tags for the statements. Mark whether it is more likely to fall or rise.

a You're angry with me, *aren't you?*   ▼

b Last night was such a hot night,

————— ?   ☐

c You couldn't help me carry this bag,

————— ?   ☐

d Tom's late again, ————— ?   ☐

e Cold for the time of year, ————— ?   ☐

f Toby hasn't drunk twelve pints of lager,

————— ?   ☐

g I'm just hopeless at telling jokes,

————— ?   ☐

h You haven't seen my pen anywhere,

————— ?   ☐

i This is a difficult exercise, ————— ?   ☐

j By the end of the film we were all in tears,

————— ?   ☐

k You wouldn't have change for a ten-pound

note, ————— ?   ☐

l We'd never seen a sunset like that before,

————— ?   ☐

2 **T 9.6** Write a sentence and a question tag for the following situations and choose the intonation pattern.

Example
You ask Tom if he could help you do your homework.
Tom, you couldn't help me with my homework, could you?   ▲

a You and a friend are looking at new cars in a car showroom. You can see that your friend really likes the red sports car.

You ————————— ?

b You think that Vanessa is going on a business trip to Rome next week, but you're not absolutely sure.

Vanessa, you ————————— ?

c You're coming out of a restaurant where you have just had a really tasteless meal with a friend.

That ————————— ?

d You can't believe that your sister has borrowed your new coat again.

You ————————— ?

e You need a neighbour to water your plants while you're away.

You ————————— ?

10

Expressing habit
get and *become*

Present and past habit

1 Tina's diary

1 **T 10.1** Read Tina's diary. Then complete the sentences using one of the words from below. Use each word or expression *once* only.

always	sometimes	frequently	usually	will
rarely	occasionally	hardly ever	used to	would

Example
Tina *always* gets up at 7 o'clock.

a She _____ has breakfast. ☐

b Uncle Jim _____ writes to Tina. ☐

c Tina _____ go to school with Fran. ☐

d The trains are _____ delayed. ☐

e The trains are _____ on time. ☐

f Tina _____ arrives at work on time. ☐

g Karen is _____ shouting at Tina. ☐

h Tina _____ goes to bed early. ☐

i Next door's cat _____ leave birds on Tina's doorstep. ☐

j Tina and her Mum _____ often watch old films on rainy Sunday afternoons. ☐

2 Tick (✓) those sentences which express past habit.

Monday September 7th

Got up at 7 o'clock. Had a slice of toast for breakfast. Got a letter from Uncle Jim in Australia, which was nice as he doesn't write that often. Work was boring, but at least Tony rang this evening and asked to take me to the cinema. Excellent! Went to bed at 10.30.

Tuesday September 8th

Got up at 7 o'clock. Had an egg for breakfast. Karen, my boss, shouted at me again for being late. I can't help it if my train's late! Watched TV in the evening with my friend Fran, and we had a bottle of wine. Fran is my oldest friend. We went to school together.

Wednesday September 9th

Got up at 7 o'clock. I didn't feel like any breakfast today. I think I drank too much wine last night. Next door's cat had caught another bird and left it on my doorstep. She does this a lot, and it's not a pleasant sight in the morning. Late for work again. Karen cross again. Had an early night. I want to look my best for Tony tomorrow.

Thursday September 10th

Got up at 7 o'clock. Had some cornflakes for breakfast. I couldn't believe it. My train was actually on time today, so for once Karen didn't shout at me. Tony took me to see a great film called The Preacher's Wife. It reminded me of an old, black and white film I'd watched years ago with Mum. We always enjoyed watching old films on rainy Sunday afternoons.

Tony kissed me goodnight and asked to see me at the weekend. I think I'm in love.

Friday September 11th

Got up at 7 o'clock. Had a boiled egg for breakfast. Karen shouted at me for being late again. Went out with Fran for a pizza, but didn't drink any wine as I want to feel my best for Tony tomorrow. Thank God it's Friday!

2 Present habit

1 T 10.2 Match a sentence in **A** with a sentence in **B**.
Use your dictionary to check any new words.

	A		B
1	She's really generous.	a	He's always working overtime.
2	He's so disorganized.	b	She never thinks before she speaks.
3	She's so fashionable.	c	He won't ever do what he's told.
4	He's so dishonest.	d	She's always buying me presents.
5	She's incredibly house-proud.	e	He's always telling lies.
6	He's really stubborn.	f	She'll only wear designer clothes.
7	She's so rude.	g	He never finishes anything he starts.
8	He's so gullible.	h	She's always dusting and polishing.
9	She's very energetic.	i	He'll believe anything you say.
10	He's very ambitious.	j	She jogs to work every day.

2 Write similar sentences to those in **B** above.
Use either the Present Simple, *always* + the Present
Continuous, or *will*.

a She adores ice-cream.

_____

b He's dreadfully big-headed.

_____

c She's very fussy about her food.

_____

d He hates all sport.

_____

e They're terrible spendthrifts.

_____

f He's a real computer freak.

_____

_____

g She's a telly addict!

_____

h He's a total pessimist.

_____

i Their children have terrible table manners.

_____

j He's such a loyal friend.

_____

3 Past habit with *used to* and *would*

1 Complete the sentences with the correct form of *used
to*, positive, question, or negative.

a There _____ be a beautiful old
building where that car park is now.

b _____ have a Saturday job when you
were at school?

c She _____ be so moody. It's only
since she lost her job.

d _____ play cricket when you were at
school?

e My grandfather never _____ get so
out of breath when he climbed the stairs.

f Julie _____ be as slim as she is now.
She's been dieting.

g Where _____ go out to eat when you
lived in Madrid?

h _____ smoke 60 cigarettes a day?
How did you give up?

2 Which of the verb forms can complete the sentences below? Tick all possible answers.

Example
We _____ Auntie Jean every time we went to London.
a ✔ *visited*   b ✔ *used to visit*   c ✔ *would visit*

1 I _____ long blonde hair when I was first married.
a ☐ *had*   b ☐ *used to have*   c ☐ *would have*

2 Pam _____ out with Andy for six months but then she ditched him.
a ☐ *went*   b ☐ *used to go*   c ☐ *would go*

3 We _____ coffee and croissants every morning for breakfast.
a ☐ *had*   b ☐ *used to have*   c ☐ *would have*

4 We _____ to each other every day when we were apart.
a ☐ *wrote*   b ☐ *used to write*   c ☐ *would write*

5 He _____ to me for 25 years and then stopped.
a ☐ *wrote*   b ☐ *used to write*   c ☐ *would write*

6 In the old days people _____ you if you were in trouble.
a ☐ *helped*   b ☐ *used to help*   c ☐ *would help*

7 I _____ living so close to the sea.
a ☐ *loved*   b ☐ *used to love*   c ☐ *would love*

8 Dave _____ Molly three times if she wanted to go out with him.
a ☐ *asked*   b ☐ *used to ask*   c ☐ *would ask*

9 I _____ questions in class. I was too shy.
a ☐ *never asked*   b ☐ *never used to ask*   c ☐ *would never ask*

4 Criticizing other people

1 Tick (✓) the sentences where the speaker is being critical of someone's behaviour.

a ☐ He watches all the sports programmes on TV.

b ☐ He's always watching sports programmes on TV.

c ☐ She'd give us extra lessons after school.

d ☐ She *would* give us extra lessons after school.

e ☐ She was always giving us extra lessons.

f ☐ She used to give us extra lessons.

g ☐ The cat always sleeps on my bed.

h ☐ The cat *will* sleep on my bed.

i ☐ The cat's always sleeping on my bed.

2 Rewrite the sentences below so that they express a criticism.

a My dad mends his motorbike in the living room.

_____

_____

b My brother leaves the cap off the toothpaste.

_____

_____

c My sister often borrows my clothes without asking.

_____

_____

d Uncle Tom smokes cigars in the kitchen.

_____

_____

e My grandpa used to chew tobacco in bed.

_____

_____

f Our great-grandma didn't use to turn on her hearing aid.

_____

_____

My Family

5 Henry's £4.5 million secret

1 Read the story of Henry Wardle. Which of the verbs in *italics* …

  1 … can change to both *would* or *used to*?
  2 … can change only to *used to*?
  3 … must stay in the Past Simple?

Put the correct number 1–3 next to the letters.

Henry's £4.5 million secret!

The villagers in Middleton, Yorkshire often (**a**) ☐ *worried* about poor old Henry Wardle. Henry, 86, (**b**) ☐ *lived* alone except for his ancient cat, Tiddles, in a tiny, one-bedroomed cottage, and always (**c**) ☐ *asked* for credit when buying cat food in the local shop. Then last month Henry (**d**) ☐ *died* leaving 4.5 million pounds in his will. The truth was that Henry was a multi-millionaire, and he (**e**) ☐ *owned* houses all over the country from which he (**f**) ☐ *made* a fortune in rent. All this came as a complete shock to his neighbours. They believed that Henry (**g**) ☐ *was* a poor window cleaner, and indeed he often (**h**) ☐ *entertained* them with tales from his window-cleaning days.

However, his brother, Mr Sam Wardle, 82, said that this was all nonsense. Henry had never been a window cleaner but had started work at the age of fourteen as a bricklayer. Then when he was 30 he (**i**) ☐ *bought* his first house, and after that he frequently (**j**) ☐ *bought* and sold houses. Sam says that his brother's only interest was making money, but he (**k**) ☐ *hated* spending it. He (**l**) ☐ *didn't spend* a penny of his own money unless he had to. Henry never once (**m**) ☐ *had* a holiday, but for many years he (**n**) ☐ *had* a girlfriend, a lady called Betty Barraclough, but he (**o**) ☐ *decided* not to marry her because a wife was too expensive.

Henry (**p**) ☐ *left* his £4,500,000 to Tiddles and a local cat charity. His friends and family received nothing.

2 Here are some sentences about Henry. Complete each gap with *one* suitable word.

  a The villagers used to _____ all Henry's lies.

  b The shopkeeper was used _____ giving Henry credit.

  c Henry _____ often talk about his work as a window cleaner.

  d In fact he _____ use to work as a window cleaner.

  e He liked making money, but he didn't _____ to like spending it.

  f Sam must have got _____ to his brother's mean ways over the years.

  g Henry was _____ buying and selling houses.

  h Tiddles _____ a lot of money from Henry.

get and become in changes of state

> ⚠ 1 Compare these sentences.
>
> *Don't worry. You'll soon **get used to** working such long hours.*
>
> *I **am used to** working long hours, I've done it for years.*
>
> *He eventually **got used to** living in a tropical climate, but it took a long time.*
>
> *I was born in India so I**'m used to** living in a hot climate.*
>
> *Get used to* means *become used to* and describes a change of state. *Be used to* describes a state.
>
> 2 *Get* can be used with other past participles and adjectives to describe changes of state.
>
> *The sea**'s getting rough**. Let's go back!*
> *We **got lost** on the mountain.*
> *We **got married** last week.*
>
> 3 *Get* can sometimes be used with an infinitive to talk about a gradual change.
>
> *As I **got to know** Paris, I started to like it more and more.*
> *I'm sure the kids will soon **get to like** each other.*
>
> The period of change doesn't have to be gradual. It can be sudden.
>
> *She'll be furious if she **gets to hear** about this.*
>
> 4 *Become* with adjectives and past participles is more formal than *get*.
>
> *The sea **was becoming** rough, so they returned to the shore.*
>
> It cannot be used with past participles which describe deliberate actions.
>
> *We became lost on the mountain.*
> **We ~~became married~~ last week.*
>
> *Become* is also used with nouns.
>
> *He **became a millionaire** at 40.*
> *I'm going to **become a model**.*

6 get, become, or be?

Complete the gaps with *get*, *become*, or *be* in the correct form and one of the words or expressions from the box.

better	clear	ready (×2)	dressed	dark	ill
tired	to like	used to	to know	a pilot	lost
upset	a bore	widespread	divorced		

a I always _____ when I watch the news. There are so many awful things happening in the world.

b It was reported that many of the guests _____ with food poisoning after the wedding reception.

c **A** How are you feeling?

 B I _____ slowly, but I still feel a bit weak.

d My little nephew is determined _____ _____ when he grows up.

e **A** Come on, Helen! Get a move on! The play starts in ten minutes.

 B I _____ in two minutes. I _____ just _____ .

 A I don't know why it takes you so long. I _____ _____ since 6.00.

f **A** Do we turn right or left at the next junction?

 B I've no idea! I think we _____ .

g **A** Did you hear that Sue and Chris _____ _____?

 B No! I don't believe it. I always thought they were the perfect couple.

h After hours of discussion it gradually _____ that those at the meeting would never reach agreement.

i I didn't like Mick at all when I first met him, but as I _____ him, I _____ him more and more. Now he's my best friend!

j If you _____ Indian food, this dish will taste very hot and spicy.

k Uncle Ted _____ a bit of _____ lately. All he talks about is how good things were in the old days when he was a young man. We're all fed up with him.

l Can we stop walking for a minute? I need a rest. I _____ .

m In summer it is still light at 9.00 in the evening, but in winter it _____ at 5.00.

n The police authorities are concerned that drug taking _____ more _____ among young people. More and more teenagers admit to trying illegal drugs.

7 Money

1 Match the words or expressions in **B** with a word or expression in **either A or C**.
Use your dictionary to help you.

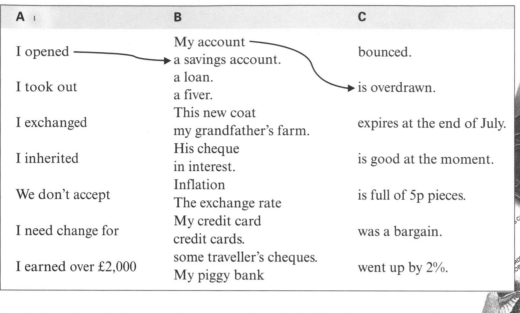

A	B	C
I opened	My account	bounced.
	a savings account.	
I took out	a loan.	is overdrawn.
	a fiver.	
I exchanged	This new coat	expires at the end of July.
	my grandfather's farm.	
I inherited	His cheque	is good at the moment.
	in interest.	
We don't accept	Inflation	is full of 5p pieces.
	The exchange rate	
I need change for	My credit card	was a bargain.
	credit cards.	
I earned over £2,000	some traveller's cheques.	went up by 2%.
	My piggy bank	

2 Read about Barnaby's trip to the supermarket. <u>Underline</u> the correct words.
Use your dictionary to look up any new words.

A lesson in thrift at the supermarket

Barnaby stood at the (**a**) *check-in/check-out* at his local supermarket listening to the *beep beep* as the assistant ran her scanner over the (**b**) *bar codes/prices* on his groceries. She (**c**) *summed/added up* his (**d**) *bill/fees/amount*. It came to £45.67 and she asked him how he would like to (**e**) *charge/pay/cost*.

Barnaby knew he didn't have much money in his bank account because his (**f**) *wages/salary/payment* hadn't gone in yet that month, and so if he paid by (**g**) *cheque/cash/instalments* he would become (**h**) *overdrawn/overdue*. So he decided to pay by credit card. However, when he opened his (**i**) *purse/wallet/handbag* he realized he had left his card at home. Also he couldn't pay (**j**) *cash/coins/money* because he only had £35.

Barnaby felt his face go red when he tried to explain his situation to the assistant. However, she was quite sympathetic. She said that this happened to lots of (**k**) *clients/customers/colleagues*. She told him that if he exchanged many of the items he had bought for the shop's own brand he would (**l**) *cut/decrease/lower* his bill by at least 25%. Barnaby thought this was an excellent idea, and set off round the store with his trolley again.

His new bill (**m**) *added/totalled/came to* only £33.50, a (**n**) *refund/saving/discount* of £12.17. Barnaby handed over his £35 and the assistant gave him £1.50 (**o**) *change/coins/cash* and his (**p**) *receipt/recipe/statement*. Barnaby thanked her profusely for all her help.

Prepositions

8 Verb + object + preposition

Put a verb in its correct form and a preposition into the gaps.

Example
He *thanked* the nurse *for* all her help.

Verb			Preposition	
thank	forgive	invest	against	into
accuse	hide	invite	at	of
brainwash	hold	model	for	on
congratulate	inherit	remind	from	to
compensate	insure	shout	in	

a You _____ me so much _____ your father. You look just like him.

b We are going to _____ all our money _____ stocks and shares.

c We have _____ our car _____ fire and theft.

d Everyone _____ me _____ passing my driving test at the fourth attempt.

e She _____ by the insurance company _____ the injuries she received in the car crash.

f My teenage daughter always _____ herself _____ her latest pop idol. She's just had a ring put through her nose, just like him.

g Don't _____ the truth _____ me. I want to know everything.

h He picked up the crying baby and _____ her tightly _____ his chest.

i We've _____ 300 guests _____ our wedding.

j I think that TV advertising _____ people _____ buying things that they don't really want.

k I didn't _____ a penny _____ my great uncle when he died.

l The spectators _____ abuse _____ the referee when he disallowed the goal.

m How can I ever _____ him _____ telling me all those lies?

n I _____ by my employers _____ stealing, which I denied strongly.

Pronunciation

9 Rhymes and limericks

1 **T 10.3** Each word in the box makes a rhyming pair with one of the words in the columns. Write the rhyming pairs next to each other.

chief	court	deaf	fool	~~good~~	mud
height	lose	knew	knows	grieve	put
reign	nude	said	pour	weight	wool

should	/ʊd/	*good*	food	/uːd/	_____
bread	/ed/	_____	leaf	/iːf/	_____
choose	/uːz/	_____	taught	/ɔːt/	_____
toes	/əʊz/	_____	chef	/ef/	_____
hate	/eɪt/	_____	through	/uː/	_____
tight	/aɪt/	_____	wore	/ɔː/	_____
full	/ʊl/	_____	brain	/eɪn/	_____
pool	/uːl/	_____	leave	/ɪːv/	_____
blood	/ʌd/	_____	foot	/ʊt/	_____

2 **T 10.4** Limericks are short poems with a distinctive rhythm. They rhyme AABBA. Here are two. Transcribe the words written in phonetic script.

THE PELICAN

A rare old bird is a pelican
His /biːk kən həʊld mɔː ðən ɪz beli kæn/

_____

He /kən teɪk ɪn ɪz bɪːk/

_____

ɪnʌf fuːd fər ə wiːk/

_____

And I'm damned if I know how the /heli kæn/

_____

THE LADY FROM TWICKENHAM

There was a young lady from Twickenham
Whose /ʃuːz wə tuː taɪt tə wɔːk kwɪk ɪn əm/

_____

She came back from a walk
/lʊkɪŋ waɪtə ðən tʃɔːk/

_____

And she /tʊk əm bəʊθ ɒf ən wəz sɪk ɪn əm/

_____

11

Hypothesis
unless, provided, in case …

Real time or unreal time?

1 Real or hypothetical past?

1 **T 11.1** The following sentences all contain verbs in the Past Simple. Read them and tick (✔) those that refer to real past time. What do the others refer to?

a ☐ **Did** you **see** Lorenzo when you **were** in Italy?

b ☐ I wish I **worked** in the open air.

c ☐ If you **didn't smoke** you wouldn't cough so much.

d ☐ When we **lived** in London we'd always travel by underground.

e ☐ I'd rather we **lived** in a small country town.

f ☐ It's time we **had** a new car.

g ☐ If only you **were** always as happy as you are today.

h ☐ Why **didn't** you **come** to the party?

2 **T 11.2** These sentences all contain verbs in the Past Perfect. Read them and tick (✔) those that express reality and cross (✘) those which don't.

a ☐ I wish **I'd said** that.

b ☐ She asked me if I **had known** her brother for a long time.

c ☐ If I **hadn't been** so nervous, I would have passed the exam.

d ☐ If only you**'d arrived** five minutes earlier.

e ☐ I woke up and realized it **had** all **been** a terrible dream.

f ☐ What if they **hadn't agreed** to give you a pay rise?

g ☐ **Had** the water **risen** just one centimetre more, our house would have been flooded.

h ☐ She told me that she**'d been given** a diamond necklace for her birthday.

3 Complete the sentences with an auxiliary verb. Note that the auxiliary verb expresses reality.

Example
I wish you didn't bite your nails, but you *do*.

a I wish I earned more, but I _____ .

b I should have listened to their advice, but I _____ .

c If only I could speak Spanish, but I _____ .

d If only he weren't so selfish, but he _____ .

e I wish my car would start, but it _____ .

f I wish you wouldn't get at me all the time, but you _____ .

g If only I hadn't been sacked, but I _____ .

h I wish I had a nice flat of my own, but I _____ .

Wishes and regrets

2 Present and past wishes

1 Use the words from the columns to make as many correct and logical sentences as you can.

I wish	you I	were could would had	come. rich.

2 <u>Underline</u> the correct alternative in the following sentences. Sometimes two are possible.

a I really wish I *can / could / was able to* speak another language.

b I wish it *wasn't / wouldn't be / isn't* so cold. I hate the winter.

c Don't you wish that you *don't / doesn't / didn't* have to go to work tomorrow?

d Our weekend away was a complete disaster. I wish we *didn't go / hadn't gone / weren't going*.

e The party was really boring after you left. We all wish you *would stay / had stayed / stayed* longer.

f I wish you *weren't speaking / didn't speak / wouldn't speak* so quickly. I can't understand a word you're saying.

g I wish I *didn't spend / wouldn't spend / hadn't spent* all my money. Now I can't afford anything to eat and I'm starving!

h Mrs Palmer wishes her grandchildren *live / lived / had lived* nearer. Then she could visit them more often.

3 Expressions of regret

1 Rewrite each sentence so it has a similar meaning to the first. Use the word in bold.

a **wish**
I'm sorry I didn't invite him to the party.

_____

b **should**
Why weren't you watching the road?

_____

c **If only**
I regret saying that to her.

_____

d **wish**
I shouldn't have hit him.

_____

e **'d rather**
I don't want you to tell her.

_____

f **wish**
I don't like it when Megan stays out so late.

_____

g **If only**
I'm really sorry we can't come to your wedding.

_____

h **should**
I regret that I didn't work harder for my exams.

_____

2 What do you imagine the people in the pictures are thinking? Write sentences to express their wishes and regrets. Use the expressions in Exercise 1.

_____

_____

_____

Third conditional

4 Making excuses

1 Rearrange the words to make excuses in the third conditional.

a wouldn't / been / if / ill / hadn't / shellfish / had / I / I / have / the

_____

_____

b phoned / had / had / if / you / have / time / would / I / the / I

_____

_____

c if / so / known / had / I / the jumper / expensive / was / wouldn't / I / bought / have / it

_____

_____

_____

d If / it / own / my / eyes / seen / with / hadn't / I / wouldn't / believed / I / have / it

_____

_____

_____

2 Complete the second sentence to express the excuse in a different way.

Example
I didn't know you had a mobile phone. I didn't contact you.
If I_'d known you had a mobile phone I could / would have contacted you_.

a I didn't send you a postcard because I didn't know your address.

If I _____

_____ a postcard.

b I didn't know when your birthday was. That's why I didn't buy you a present.

If _____

_____ .

c I'm sorry I'm late. I forgot to set my alarm clock.

If _____

_____ .

d I broke the speed limit because I was taking my wife to the hospital.

If _____

_____ .

5 May's disastrous day `T 11.3`

A disastrous day for May

LAST SUNDAY NIGHT May forgot to set her alarm clock, so she overslept and was an hour late for work. May's boss, Ms Collins, called her into the office and told her that because she was late again she couldn't go on a planned business trip to New York the following week. Ms Collins said that she'd decided to send a more reliable person. May was so upset about missing her business trip that she locked herself in the ladies' toilet and cried her heart out. Also, she completely forgot that she had arranged to meet her boyfriend, Ben, for lunch at an Italian restaurant.

1 May Brown is a sales executive for a leading cosmetics company. Read about her disastrous day and complete the sentences below.

a May wouldn't have overslept if _____

_____

b Her business trip wouldn't have been cancelled if

_____ .

c If she hadn't been so upset, she _____

_____ toilet and she _____

_____ Ben for lunch.

d If she'd met Ben for lunch, _____

_____ .

e If she hadn't cried so much, _____

_____

f She could have driven home if _____

Eventually she dried her eyes and returned to her desk. She looked at her computer screen, it was totally out of focus. She asked her colleague at the next desk if he could help her put it right, but he said that he couldn't see anything wrong with it. Then May realized what had happened. The computer was all right, but she wasn't. She'd lost one of her contact lenses in the toilet.

At last the day ended. Without her contact lens May had to get the bus home and leave her car at work because she couldn't see to drive. She waited at the bus stop for over an hour in the pouring rain and didn't get home until 8 o'clock. There, she was greeted by a message from Ben on her answering machine.

He was very angry and reminded her that this was the third time she had forgotten to meet him. He said that she clearly didn't care for him and that this was the end of their relationship. May was heartbroken. In tears for the second time that day, she decided to go to bed before anything else could go wrong. However, she forgot to feed the cat.

The next day, with a streaming cold, she went downstairs to make herself a cup of tea and found bird feathers everywhere. The poor cat had resorted to desperate measures to get food. It had eaten the budgie! Poor budgie! May went back to bed and pulled the covers over her head.

g If she'd driven home, _____

_____ .

h She wouldn't have caught cold if _____

_____ .

i Her boyfriend wouldn't have ended their

relationship if _____

_____ .

j If she'd remembered to feed the cat, _____

_____ .

2 **T 11.4** Complete the phone conversation that May had with Ben the next day.

M Ben, I can't tell you how sorry I am. *Atishoo!* Everything went wrong for me yesterday. The last straw was this morning when I found the cat had eaten the budgie. And in a way that was your fault.

B What?! What are you talking about?

M Well, if you hadn't _____

_____ .

B So it's *my* fault you didn't feed the cat? Come off it, May! Whose fault was it that you forgot to meet me for lunch?

M Well, that was Ms Collins' fault. If she hadn't

_____

_____ .

B And *why* did she cancel your business trip? Whose fault was that? Mine or Ms Collins'?

M Well, I suppose that *was* my fault. You see, I didn't set my alarm, so I overslept and I was late again for work.

B Ah! Now I understand everything. If you'd

remembered _____

_____ .

M OK, OK I'm sorry. *Atishooo!* It's all my fault. *Atishooo!* But Ben, I feel so ill.

B You sound dreadful. How did you get such a bad cold?

M That's another story. Come round and see me and I'll tell you and I promise not to feel too sorry for myself. *Atishooo!*

All conditionals

6 Revision of all conditionals

Put the verb in brackets in the correct tense to form either the first, second, third, or zero conditional. There are also some examples of mixed conditionals.

a If I still _____ (feel) sick, I _____ (not go) on holiday next weekend.

b You make such delicious chocolate cakes!

   If you _____ (sell) them, you _____ (make) a fortune.

c Hello, Liz. Are you still looking for Pat?

   If I _____ (see) her, I _____ (tell) her you want to speak to her.

d If Alice _____ (go) to Exeter University, she _____ (not met) her husband, Andrew.

e 'Does she love him?' 'Of course she does. If she _____ (not love) him, she _____ (not marry) him.'

f If you _____ (buy) two apples, you _____ (get) one free.

g **A** What _____ you _____ (do) if you _____ (see) a ghost?

   B I _____ (run) a mile!

h We're lost. If we _____ (bring) the map with us, we _____ (know) where we are.

i You were very lucky to catch the fire in time. If you _____ (not have) a smoke alarm fitted, the house _____ (burn down).

j You were very rude to Max. If I _____ (be) you, I _____ (apologize).

k Ashley is allergic to cheese. If he _____ (eat) cheese, he _____ (get) an awful rash.

l We've run out of petrol. If you _____ (listen) to me sometimes instead of being so stubborn, you _____ (hear) me saying that we were getting low. Then we _____ (not be) stuck here.

Ways of introducing conditionals

1 Conditionals can be introduced in a variety of ways other than *if*.

   unless
   Unless means *if not* in the sense of *except if*.
   > We'll go swimming **unless** it rains.
   > **Unless** there's a strike, I'll be at work tomorrow.

   in case
   In case means the first action is a precaution. It happens because the second action *might* happen. Compare these two sentences.
   > I'll take my umbrella **in case** it rains.
   > I'll take my umbrella **if** it rains.

   supposing / suppose / imagine
   These mean the same as *imagine if ...?* or *what if ...?* The condition is more improbable, so they are more often found with the second and third conditionals. They come at the beginning of a sentence.
   > **Supposing** you could fly, where would you go?
   > **Imagine** you were rich, what would you buy?

   provided / providing (that), as / so long as
   These mean the same as *on condition that*. They are more often found with the first conditional.
   > I'll go to the party, **provided** you go.
   > I'll be happy **as long as** I have you.

2 In more formal styles *if* can be dropped and the auxiliary verb inverted.
   > **Were** you to **question** me about the matter, I would deny all knowledge.
   > **Had** I **known** that he was a journalist, I would have said nothing.
   > **Should** the meeting **last** longer than expected, I'll have to cancel my dinner engagement.

7 Words other than *if*

1 Underline the correct word.

   a *Providing / Supposing* there were no more wars, wouldn't that be wonderful?

   b I'm going to take a cushion to the concert, *in case / unless* the seats are hard.

   c We'll miss the beginning of the film *so long as / unless* you hurry.

   d *Providing / In case* you behave yourself, you can come to the party with us.

   e *Suppose / Were* I your teacher, I'd make sure that everyone did the homework.

f He will never be happy *as long as/unless* he's got that boring job.

g *Had/Supposing* I understood the problem, I'd have done something about it.

h *Should/Provided* you fail to pay this bill, court action will be taken.

2 Rewrite these sentences using the words in brackets.

a I won't come if they don't invite me. (unless)

_____

b What would you do if he left you? (supposing)

_____

_____

c If you join the tennis club, I will too.
(provided that)

_____

_____

d We're going to install a smoke alarm. There may be a fire. (in case)

_____

_____

e She won't get that job if she doesn't learn to speak French. (unless)

_____

_____

f If the lifeguard hadn't been there, what would have happened? (imagine)

_____

_____

g I won't go out this evening. Paul might ring.
(in case)

_____

_____

h I'll come at 8.00 if that's all right with you.
(as long as)

_____

_____

8 Poor rich Mr Briggs

Read about Mr Amos Briggs, a most unfortunate lottery winner. Put *one* word only into each gap.

Poor rich Mr Briggs!

TWO YEARS AGO I WON £1 MILLION ON THE LOTTERY and to be honest now I really (**a**) _____ I hadn't. I know I've got a six-bedroom house with a swimming pool and tennis court, and a Mercedes convertible. All of this is wonderful (**b**) _____ that the rest of your life is OK, but this wretched money has brought me nothing but unhappiness.

Three months ago my wife, Joanie, left me and took our two children. She warned me that (**c**) _____ I spent more time with her and the children and less time spending money, she (**d**) _____ leave, but I didn't listen. I (**e**) _____ have realized what was happening, but I didn't. I was too busy organizing the building of this house. I just took my family for granted. If (**f**) _____ I hadn't been so self-centred! I miss them so much. There's no point in having all this wealth (**g**) _____ you don't have anyone to share it with. I live alone in this huge house. Most days I just sit watching TV and playing computer games. I jump up every time the phone rings in (**h**) _____ it's Joanie, but it never is. She says she will never come back (**i**) _____ if I beg her, but I still live in hope.

I don't go out much. I (**j**) _____ go for a drive in my wonderful car if I was allowed to, but I was caught speeding, and now I'm banned from driving for a year. If I hadn't felt so depressed I wouldn't have (**k**) _____ speeding. It's all a chain reaction. I wouldn't (**l**) _____ depressed now if Joanie (**m**) _____ left me, and she (**n**) _____ never have left if I (**o**) _____ won the stupid lottery. My life is a total mess.

Vocabulary

9 Physical appearance or personality?

1 Are these adjectives connected with physical appearance or personality? Write them in the correct column. Careful! There is *one* that can go in both columns.

bespectacled	moody	freckled	two-faced
big-headed	brainy	graceful	wrinkled
quick-tempered	skinny	nosy	bald
absent-minded	cheeky	spotty	well-built
narrow-minded	affectionate	smart	curly
hard-hearted	agile	chubby	

Physical appearance	Personality

2 The words in bold are all parts of the body, and usually used as nouns. They can also be used as verbs. Match a verb with a line on the right.

	arm	out the books to the class
	back	the bill for the meal
	elbow	the material gently
	eye	someone with suspicion
	finger	someone out of the way
to	**foot**	out of an agreement/ the car out of the garage
	hand	a country against the threat of war
	head	the ball into the net
	shoulder	through a book quickly
	thumb	the line in a job or organization
	toe	the responsibility/blame

3 Complete the sentences with a 'body' verb in its correct form.

a The teacher _____ out the exam papers and told the class to begin writing.

b I managed to _____ my way to the front of the crowd, so I got a good view of the procession.

c I haven't read the magazine yet, I just

_____ through it to see if there were any interesting pictures.

d We all _____ the new member of class with curiosity. We were eager to see what she was like.

e They ordered the most expensive things on the menu

because they knew that I _____ the bill.

f In the final seconds of the match Benson

_____ the ball into the back of the net making it one–nil.

g The soldiers _____ with rifles and ready for battle.

h In our company all employees have to

_____ the line or be sacked.

i I love the feeling of real silk. I can't stop

_____ it.

j We've just learnt that the investors _____ out of the deal, so now we don't know where the money is coming from.

k I'd hate to be Prime Minister. I don't think I could

_____ the responsibility of making so many important decisions.

Phrasal verbs

10 Nouns from phrasal verbs

> 1 There are many nouns formed from phrasal verbs. Sometimes the verb element comes first, and sometimes it comes second.
>
> **make**-up   down**fall**   **hang**over   up**bring**ing
> **draw**back   out**break**   **take**away   by-**pass**
>
> 2 Sometimes the noun is related to the phrasal verb, and sometimes it isn't.
>
> *I use a lot of **make-up**.*
> *She **made up** her face very carefully.* = related
>
> *The main **drawback** to your plan is that it's too expensive.* (*drawback* = disadvantage)
> ***Draw back** the curtains and let the sunshine in.* (*draw back* = open)

Put one of the nouns in the box into each gap.

outcome	breakthrough	by-pass	outbreak
hangover	takeaway	check-up	breakdown
comeback	feedback	outlook	downfall

a The _____ of communication between management and workers means the strike will continue.

b His career as a pop singer has suffered over the past few years, but now with a new album and a world tour, he's trying to make a _____ .

c I had too much beer last night. Today I've got a _____ .

d I go to the dentist twice a year for a _____ .

e The _____ of the election is that Labour has a majority of 90.

f There used to be so much traffic going through our town, but since the _____ was built we only have local traffic.

g The weather should be stable over the next few days, and the _____ for the weekend is warm and sunny.

h There has been an _____ of food poisoning as a result of people eating contaminated meat pies.

i There has been a significant _____ in the search to find a cure for the common cold.

j Producers often ask their customers to complete questionnaires on their products, because they need to get _____ to see what the people think.

k 'What's for supper?' 'A Chinese _____ .'

l He used to be a highly successful businessman, but he lost the lot. Greed was his _____ .

Pronunciation

11 Ways of pronouncing -ea-

1 There are several different ways of pronouncing -*ea*-. Look at the examples in the boxes.

/e/ bread	/iː/ meat	/ɪə/ fear
/eə/ wear	/eɪ/ break	/ɜː/ learn

2 **T 11.5** Put the following words into the correct column according to the pronunciation of -*ea*-. Careful! Words marked with an asterisk* have two meanings and two pronunciations.

dear	tear*	scream	steak	breath
breathe	breadth	spear	thread	bear
cease	cheat	clear	deaf	death
earth	beast	breast	beard	pearl
pear	heal	health	great	gear
hearse	jealous	yearn	lead*	leap
leapt	meant	reason	search	swear
theatre	weary	weapon		

12

Noun phrases
Adding emphasis
Nouns in groups (2)

Noun phrases

1 Adding information before and after a noun

1 Look at the picture and complete the sentences.

a There's a woman *wearing a* hat _____ pram.

b I can see a boy _____ dog.

c A man _____ bench _____ newspaper
_____ sandwich.

d There's a gardener _____ head _____ grass.

e A family _____ under a tree _____ picnic.

f I can see _____ van _____ queue.

g There are _____ on the lake.

h Some men _____ side _____ lake.

i There's a boy _____ hill _____ kite.

j I can see a boy _____ bike _____ past the lake.

2 Complete the compound nouns that
you can see in the picture.

a lawn _____

b _____ bin

c _____ racquet

d _____ posts

e _____ barrow

f _____ van

g _____ boat

h _____ rod

i mountain _____

j roller_____

3 Rewrite the short sentences to form one longer sentence.

a I'm going on holiday. It will last for two weeks. It'll be quite an adventure. We're going to drive through the Sahara Desert.

_____

_____

b The judge gave her a sentence. He sent her to prison for five years. She had kidnapped a millionaire's son.

_____

_____

c She's going to do a course. It will take three years. She'll be studying modern languages. It's at Oxford University.

_____

_____

d Mercedes have brought out a new car. It's a sports car. It has two doors. Its top speed is 150 miles per hour.

_____

_____

2 Articles

1 Put *a*, *the*, or nothing (the zero article) into the gaps.

a Excuse me! Is there _____ bank near here?

b 'I haven't got any money.' 'I'm going to _____ bank. I'll get you some.'

c Has _____ postman been this morning?

d My brother works as _____ postman.

e We've seen a house we want to move to. It's got _____ views over fields, and there's _____ lovely garden at _____ back.

f 'Where's Nick?' 'In _____ garden.'

g I bought _____ gun to protect myself against _____ burglars.

h Tony joined _____ Army because he likes playing with _____ guns.

i We went out for _____ meal last night. _____ food was excellent. I don't usually like _____ Chinese food, but _____ duck was superb.

2 **T 12.1** Fill the gaps in the newspaper article with *a*, *an*, *the*, *his*, or nothing.

Hero saves mid-air overdose victim with sugar

(a) _____ airline passenger saved (b) _____ life of (c) _____ man who had taken (d) _____ drugs overdose by using (e) _____ sugar sachets as (f) _____ antidote.

Simon Greenway, 19, (g) _____ former Army paramedic, used 22 of (h) _____ sachets and five pints of water to dilute (i) _____ valium and vodka taken by (j) _____ passenger.

(k) _____ passenger, (l) _____ student from Norway, had collapsed shortly after (m) _____ British Airways flight left Bucharest for (n) _____ three-hour flight to (o) _____ Heathrow Airport.

Mr Greenway said, 'I saw this bloke staggering around before we got on (p) _____ plane, and I just thought he was drunk. But when we were in (q) _____ air I noticed (r) _____ white powder around (s) _____ lips. Then he fell over into my lap, and he said something about wanting to kill himself. (t) _____ captain asked to be kept in (u) _____ touch in case we needed to make (v) _____ emergency landing, but I

knew we didn't have much time. The Army taught us how to deal with (w) _____ people who have overdosed. The cabin crew are trained in (x) _____ first aid, but after speaking to the head steward it became clear that I had more training, so I took over. When we landed, (y) _____ crew thanked me and gave me a bottle of champagne, but I don't drink and I have given it to my friends.'

(z) _____ British Airways spokesman said, 'We are grateful to Simon for his quick thinking and initiative.'

3 Determiners

Choose which words fit the sentences.

a I have three dogs. *All/Every* of them love going for a walk, but *neither/none* of them likes being brushed.

b You can borrow *either/each* the Renault or the Rover. They're *all/both* in the garage.

c My two daughters are *each/both* good at languages, but *none/neither* of them can do maths at all.

d I have a shower *every/each* day.

e I've got thirty people in my class, and *every/each* student is special to me.

f 'How much are the roses?' 'One pound *either/each*.'

g I have *any/no* idea how I spend all my money. At the end of *every/either* month, it's all gone.

h I know *every/each* word of his songs by heart.

i There are fifteen rooms in this hotel. *Each/Every* room is a little different.

j You can have *either/each* an orange or an apple, but you can't have *either/both*.

k 'Tea or coffee?' '*Either/Neither*, thanks. I've got to rush.'

l 'Red wine or white?' '*Either/Neither*, whichever is open.'

m I know *either/both* Robert and his brother, but I don't like *both/either* of them.

n 'Can you help me with my homework?' 'Sure. *None/No* problem.'

o I have four brothers. *Every/Each* of us is different.

4 Demonstratives

Put *this*, *that*, *these*, or *those* into each gap.

a _____ shoes are killing me. I can't wait to take them off.

b (On the phone) Hello. _____ is Beth. Can I speak to Kate?

c _____ was a wonderful film, wasn't it?

d I knew Jenny at university. In _____ days she had long blonde hair.

e 'Anything else?' 'No, _____'s all for today, thanks.'

f Well, _____'ll be £5.50, please.

g I can't get _____ ring off my finger. It's stuck.

h You just can't get proper cheese _____ days.

i Come here and tidy up _____ mess right now!

j Listen to _____ . It says in the paper that life's been found on Mars.

k Did you ever hear from _____ girl you met on holiday last year?

l I was in the pub last night when _____ bloke came up to me and hit me.

m 'I got a parking fine today.' '_____'ll teach you a lesson.'

n Who were _____ people you were talking to last night?

o What was _____ noise? Didn't you hear it?

Adding emphasis

5 Emphatic structures

Rewrite the sentences, making them more emphatic.

a I love the seasons in England.

What <u>I love</u> about England <u>is the seasons</u> .

b Where does he get his money from? I don't understand this.

The thing _____

is where _____ .

c She has a sense of humour. I like this about her.

What _____ .

d I don't like the dark winter evenings.

It's _____ .

e Those children need firm guidance.

What _____ .

f Jenny always has to know best. I don't like this about her.

The thing _____

is the way _____ .

g I don't want money. I want love.

It isn't _____ .

h John never buys you a drink. I can't stand this.

What _____

is the fact that _____ .

i Kathy's sincere. You have to remember this about her.

The thing _____

_____ .

j He's jealous because I'm rich and he isn't.

It's the fact _____

_____ .

6 Emphasis in speaking

T 12.2 Mark where the main stress is in **B**'s replies.

a **A** Why didn't you do your homework last night?

   ●

B I did do it.

b **A** Who made this mark on the carpet?

B I did it. Sorry.

c **A** Did you know that John and Mary are coming tonight?

B I knew John was coming.

d **A** Did you know that John and Mary are coming tonight?

B I knew that ages ago.

e **A** Who told Ann that I smashed her car?

B I didn't tell her.

f **A** I wish you hadn't told Ann I smashed her car.

B I didn't tell her.

g **A** I lost all my money playing cards.

B I told you.

h **A** You don't like Mike and Annie, do you?

B I like Annie.

i **A** Why don't you like Annie?

B I do like Annie. I think she's great.

j **A** I feel so sorry for Annie. Nobody likes her.

B I like her.

7 Word order

Correct the mistakes in word order in the sentences.

a In the middle of winter I was born in 1981.

_____

b A new car she bought with the money in his will her father had left her.

_____

_____

c With a limp he walked, because playing football his leg he had hurt.

_____

_____

d Usually at Tesco's I go shopping because are lower the prices.

_____

_____

e Early I go shopping on Saturday morning, before arrives everyone else.

_____

_____

f I'm going today to London to buy for Jack a new coat.

_____

_____

g Immediately in the bank you should put your money.

_____

_____

h To France we went on holiday last year unfortunately but was awful the weather.

_____

_____

i Quickly she tidied up her flat, because were coming to stay her parents.

_____

_____

j Never I'll understand why so passionately she loves him.

_____

_____

8 The passive voice

Some of these sentences would be better in the active voice, and some would be better in the passive. Rewrite those which you think need correcting.

a Many of van Gogh's most famous paintings were completed in Arles in 1888, including *Sunflowers*. Just two years later he was shot by himself at the age of 37. During his lifetime, only one of his pictures was sold by him. Today his art work is among the highest priced in the world. In 1989 somebody bought *Irises* for $53.9 million.

_____

_____

_____

_____

_____

_____

_____

b A secretary has invited me to Buckingham Palace to collect an award for a book that was written by me a few years ago.

_____

_____

c A scientist discovered penicillin in 1929. Since then, many lives have been saved by it.

_____

_____

d Scientists working in America have discovered a drug that prevents the common cold. They will now produce the drug commercially, and it should be available soon.

_____

_____

_____

Nouns in groups

1 There are three main ways that we can put nouns together.

noun + noun	noun + 's + noun
post office	*my wife's sister*
sunrise	*the doctor's surgery*
headache	*the dog's bowl*
face-lift	

noun + preposition + noun
the end of the garden
a story about compassion
the arrival of the police

2 Sometimes more than one structure can be used.

the Prime Minister's arrival
  the arrival of the Prime Minister

the floor of the living room
  the living room floor

the car door handle
  the handle on the car door

But usually only one pattern is possible.

the back of the car   *~~the car back~~*
            ~~the car's back~~

3 Sometimes there is a change in meaning.

the cat's food
  = the food that belongs to one particular cat
  The dog has eaten the cat's food.

cat food = food for cats in general
  Can you buy some more cat food when you go out?

4 We use the noun + noun pattern (compound nouns) for everyday established combinations. We talk about *a love film*, *a war film*, *a horror film*, but not *~~a horse film~~*. We usually prefer the pattern with a preposition in such cases – *a film about horses*.

9 Combining nouns

Combine the words in brackets using one of the three patterns. Sometimes there is more than one possibility.

a Your coat's on the _____ (back, chair).

b You've just spilt the _____ (milk, cat).

c Can you buy some _____ (paper, toilet)? We've run out.

d I never listened to my _____ (advice, parents).

e Can you buy a _____ (wine, bottle) to have with supper?

f What did that _____ (road, sign) say? Did you see it?

g It's such a mess in here. There are empty _____ _____ (wine, bottles) everywhere.

h The _____ (Prime Minister, duties) include entertaining heads of state.

i The _____ (my shoe, heel) has come off.

j Can I borrow your _____ (brush, hair)?

k What happened at the _____ _____ (film, end)?

l Here is _____ (today, news).

m Where is the nearest _____ (Underground, station)?

n It's my _____ (anniversary, parents, wedding) next week.

o The _____ (company, success) is due to its efficiency.

p I've got a _____ (fortnight, holiday) next month.

q The _____ (government, economic policy) is confusing.

r My children go to the local _____ (school, state).

s The annual _____ (rate, inflation) is about 4%.

t Are there any _____ (coffee, cups) in your bedroom? There are none in the kitchen.

u Do you want a _____ (coffee, cup)?

Vocabulary

10 Hot verbs *set* and *break*

1 Which words and expressions go with *set*, and which go with *break*? Tick the correct column.

set		break
	off on a journey	
	a bone skiing	
	a bone in plaster	
	fire to sth	
	your alarm clock	
	the sound barrier	
	the law	
	a good example	
	a new world record	
	the old world record	
	a promise	
	someone's heart	
	your heart on doing sth	
	the speed limit	

2 Complete the sentences with one of the combinations from Exercise 1. Put the verbs in the correct form.

a Teachers should _____ to their students. They should be punctual, professional, and well-mannered.

b You're doing sixty miles per hour in a built-up area. Slow down! You're _____ .

c We have to be up at 6.00 tomorrow morning. I'll _____ for 5.45.

d After fifteen years of marriage she left him for another man. It _____, and he never really got over it.

e I was cooking some chips when the frying pan was knocked over, and I _____ the kitchen.

f Anyone who rides a motorbike without a helmet is _____ .

g 'What time do we need _____ ?' 'The plane leaves at 10.00, so we should leave here at about 8.00.'

h Woods has run the 100 metres in 8.5 seconds! He's _____ by 0.7 of a second.

i Lane has jumped an incredible 3.6 metres! She's _____ !

j I _____ my arm when I fell off my horse. When the doctor _____, I screamed with the pain.

k If you say you're going to do something, you must do it. You should never _____ .

l Concorde can only go at full speed over the sea. When it _____, there is a huge sonic boom.

m We've found the house of our dreams. We've _____ moving there, but I don't know if we'll get it.

Prepositions

11 Noun + prepositions

Put a preposition or a combination of prepositions into each gap.

a After running up the stairs, I was _____ breath.

b You make some silly mistakes, but _____ general your work has been good.

c I went on holiday _____ my own, because sometimes I like to be _____ myself.

d I got a cheque _____ £500 in the post.

e There has been a rise _____ the number of violent crimes.

f The difference _____ you and me is that I don't mind hard work.

g I can think of no reason _____ her strange behaviour.

h It took a long time to find a solution _____ the problem.

i I need some information _____ global warming.

j I'm having trouble _____ my car. It won't start in the mornings.

k In the accident there was quite a bit of damage _____ my car.

l Investigators are trying to find the cause _____ the accident.

m I'll do my homework now. No, _____ second thoughts, I'll do it tomorrow.

n Did you get an invitation _____ Harry's wedding?

o I don't see James any more. I haven't been _____ touch with him for years.

Pronunciation

12 Nouns and verbs

1 **T 12.3** In the group of words in the chart, the nouns end in an unvoiced sound (/s/, /f/, /θ/), and the verbs end in a voiced sound (/z/, /v/, /ð/).

Complete the chart with the words and the phonetics. Sometimes the vowel sound changes, and sometimes the spelling changes.

Noun	Verb
advice	/ədvaɪz/
	to use
abuse	
/bɪli:f/	
	/rɪli:v/
grief	
/ɪkskjʊ:s/	
breath	
	to halve
/haʊs/	
safe	
	/beɪð/

2 **T 12.4** Complete the sentences with one of the words in Exercise 1.

a It is my personal _____ that the man accused of the crime is innocent.

b Let me listen to your chest. Take a deep _____ and say 'Ah'.

c You should put your valuables in the hotel _____ .

d Drug _____ is a terrible problem all over the world.

e I know it isn't good for your skin, but I love sun _____ .

f I've been so worried about you! It's such a _____ to see you at last!

g 'What are we going to do with this cake?' 'Cut it in two. You take _____ and I'll take _____ .'

h Can you show me how to _____ this new coffee machine?

i The refugees are _____ in temporary accommodation.

j She apologized for her behaviour, and said it was because she'd had a lousy day at work, but that's no _____ for breaking all the plates.

k People need time to _____ after the death of someone they love.

l Take my _____ . Never marry for money. Marry for love.

Key

1 Identifying tenses
Exercise 1
a is walking
b walked
c 'd been walking
d had taken
e was taken
f 'll take
g 've had
h 'll be having
i were having
j is freshly made
k 'll have made
l 's been made
m 're being washed
n had been washed/ was washed
o 've been washing
p will have been sold
q sells
r will be sold/ 's going to be sold
s will have been teaching
t were being taught

Exercise 2
ACTIVE

	Simple	Continuous
Present	sells	is walking
Past	walked	were having
Future	will take	will be having
Present Perfect	have had	have been washing
Past Perfect	had taken	had been walking
Future Perfect	will have made	will have been teaching

PASSIVE

	Simple	Continuous
Present	is made	are being washed
Past	was taken	were being taught
Future	will be sold	
Present Perfect	has been made	
Past Perfect	had been washed	
Future Perfect	will have been sold	

2 Correcting mistakes
a ✔
b Manchester United <u>are playing</u> really well at the moment. …
c I've heard you<u>'re going to</u> have a baby!/you<u>'re having</u> a baby! …
d ✔
e When I was a little girl, I <u>always spent</u> my …
f I<u>'ve been going out</u> with Paul …
g … Perhaps I<u>'ll get</u> him …
h ✔
i A … strike <u>has been called</u> by …
j … and <u>deserved</u> to pass …

3 Choosing the right tense
a 've been looking/was looking
b wonder/'m wondering/ wondered/was wondering
c went
d 'd never been

e was doing/did
f got
g did you feel
h 's been
i 've visited
j felt
k was travelling
l have been learning/are learning
m 're looking forward
n is hoping/hopes
o will that be
p will be able
q produces
r 've been
s 'll get
t 've discussed

4 Active or passive?
Exercise 1
a Volvos aren't made in Norway.
b Our house was built in the 17th century.
c Has your bedroom been decorated?
d My bedroom's being decorated …
e While … was being built …
f … our house had been burgled.
g She won't be recognized …

Exercise 2
a were caught   were leaving/left
b arrived   had caught
c are emptied
d hadn't been delivered
e has been missing
f don't you like   love   're going to see
g were driving   were overtaken
h had been snowing
i arrive   'll be picked up

5 At home on a train
Exercise 1
a don't live
b has travelled
c is made
d 've lived/ 've been living
e didn't want
f saw
g fell
h bought
i had already done
j we're still making
k have been removed
l paid
m were offered
n 'm discovering
o was built
p 've worked/ 're working/ have been working
q 'll ever sell
r will remain/ remains

Exercise 2
a Do they live in a caravan?
b How long have they lived/been living there?
c Who did they buy it from?
d How much did they pay for their house?
e How much were they recently offered for the house?
f Where and when was it built?
g Are they still working on the house?
h Will they ever sell the house?

6 have, be, or do?
a has (A)
b did (F)
c have (F)
d 've (A)
e is/was (F) has/had (F)
f didn't (A)
g done (F)
h does (A)
i was (A)
j is (A) being (A)
k doing (F) to have (F)
l been (A)
'm (F)

7 Forms of have and have got
Exercise 1
a '… have you got/do you have a …'
'… I'm having …'
'… I've got/have … to have …'
b '… have you got/do you have …'
'… I haven't/don't …'
'… had …'
'… haven't got/don't have …'
c '… had …'
'… had …'
'… Will you have to …'
d 'Have you got/do you have …'
'No, we haven't/don't. Have/do you?'
'… I've had … I've got/have …'
'… to have …'
e '… We've got to/have to …'
'… haven't got/don't have …'
'… had … Have …'
f … having … I've had … haven't had …

Exercise 2
a She hasn't got …
b I don't usually have …
c I haven't got/don't have …
d They aren't having …
e We didn't have …
f I don't have to …
g I didn't have to …

Exercise 3
a What colour eyes has she got?
b What time do you usually have breakfast?
c How much money do you have?
d What are they having a row about?
e Did you have a good time on holiday?
f How many hours a day do you have to work?
g What time did you have to get up this morning?

8 Rooms and their contents
Kitchen: taps sink dishwasher scales breadbin tin opener cat flap tea towel high chair Welsh dresser

Living room: French windows armchair sofa rug drinks cabinet magazine rack ornaments

Bedroom: chest of drawers dressing table cot duvet wardrobe pillow ornaments sheets rug quilt

Bathroom: shower curtain towel rail washbasin bidet taps scales flannel towel

9 house and home idioms
Exercise 1
a He's got a huge appetite.
b They have a very good relationship.
c I could shop for a very long time.
d The drinks are free.
e The musical was a success.
f The pictures made me realize fully the horrors of the famine.
g Mum earns the money in our family.

h Haig managed to win, although it wasn't easy.

Exercise 2
a When I saw her empty cat basket it really brought home the fact I'd never see her again.
b We all got on like a house on fire.
c They eat us out of house and home.
d Apparently, it brought the house down.
e I could dance until the cows come home.

10 Literal and idiomatic
Exercise 1
a out
b away
c down
d off
e down
f off on
g out
h back
i in
j away

Exercise 2
a fell out (L)
fell out (I)
b put up (I)
put up (L)
c 've sorted out (L)
sort it out (I)
d stand up (L)
stand up (I)
e Hold on (I)
hold on (L)
f take it off (L)
take off (I)
g picked it up (I)
pick him up (L)

11 Vowel sounds and spelling
Exercise 1
a friend
b English
c cheese
d month
e took
f huge
g crash
h shock
i thought
j shirt
k chart
l temper

Exercise 2
/e/	l<u>e</u>tter	w<u>ea</u>ther	br<u>ea</u>kfast	head
/ɪ/	sick	w<u>o</u>men	b<u>u</u>sy	b<u>ui</u>lding
/iː/	tree	jeans	h<u>ea</u>t	mach<u>i</u>ne
/ʌ/	hug	m<u>o</u>ther	fun	w<u>o</u>rry
/ʊ/	good	w<u>o</u>man	could	p<u>u</u>llover
/uː/	cool	r<u>oo</u>f	suit	can<u>oe</u>
/æ/	camp	f<u>a</u>mily	<u>a</u>ccent	f<u>a</u>n
/ɒ/	log	odd	s<u>au</u>sage	want
/ɔː/	horse	walk	d<u>au</u>ghter	floor
/ɜː/	<u>ea</u>rly	work	s<u>ea</u>rch	worm
/ɑː/	p<u>a</u>rty	f<u>a</u>ther	ban<u>a</u>na	g<u>a</u>rden
/ə/	lett<u>e</u>r	b<u>a</u>nana	f<u>a</u>ther	m<u>a</u>chine

Exercise 3
a Learning a foreign language is very useful.
b It's important to have a good dictionary.
c English spelling isn't easy.
d It's good to keep lists of vocabulary.
e Grammar doesn't have to be boring.
f Everyone wants to speak English fluently.

1 Present Perfect simple or continuous?
Exercise 1
a I've written to Auntie Fay to wish her a happy birthday.
I've been writing my essay all morning.
b I've lost my car keys.
I've been losing weight recently.

c They've missed the train.
They've been missing you lots, so come home soon.

d She's been talking on the phone for ages.
She's talked about this subject before.

e Paula's been leaving work late all this week.
Paula's left work early today to meet her uncle.

f The cat's been going next door to have its dinner.
The cat's gone upstairs.

g He's had a heart attack.
He's been having second thoughts about accepting the job.

h I've been saving up to buy a new stereo.
I've saved up about £200.

i I've been swimming which is why my hair is wet.
I've swum twenty lengths today.

j I've been finding it difficult to concentrate recently.
I've found my cheque book at last.

Exercise 2
a 's been snowing
b have you travelled
c have lived 've been trying haven't managed
d have been arguing
e 've eaten
f have been running
g 's been crying 's failed
h 've been sunbathing

2 Present Perfect/Past Simple
a Which school did he go to?
b How long has he known Julian?
Since he was 11 years old.
c How long has he been married to Maria?
d What did he do/was he doing in Argentina?
He taught/was teaching English.
e When did he return to England?
After his son was born.
f How many times did he work as a sales representative?
g Where did he move to after Caroline was born?
h How long has he been selling clothes?
Since he was fifty-five years old.
i Has Paul had a successful career?
No, he hasn't, because he's now selling clothes at Peckham market.

3 World's highest dustman
Exercise 1
a lives
b has already made
c aims/'s aiming
d was working
e heard
f was looking
g has found
h came
i has collected
j has been preparing
k 's training
l succeeds

Exercise 2
a 'm beginning
b 've done
c feel
d 've been learning/
m try/'m trying/
 've been trying
n 's snowed/
 's been snowing
o are sunbathing/

've learned
e isn't/hasn't been
f 've slept/'ve been sleeping
g 're staying
h dream
i haven't seen
j feels
k 've been telling/ tell
l 's been/is

have been sunbathing
p are checking/ have been checking
q mentioned
r are thinking/ were thinking
s get
t make
u get up
v to be lying

4 Present Perfect passive
a A yachtsman has been rescued in the Pacific.
b Valuable jewels have been stolen from Harrods.
c The missing boy has been found alive.
d MPs have been given a huge pay rise.
e Ten people have been killed by a tornado in Texas.
f An ancient tomb has been discovered in Egypt.
g 2,000 people have been made redundant at British Aerospace.
h A cure has been discovered for teenage acne.

5 have something done
Exercise 1
a I had one hundred copies of my report printed.
b She wants to have her ears pierced.
c I'm going to have my eyes tested.
d They've had their leaking roof fixed.
e We haven't had the photocopier mended yet.

Exercise 2 (Sample answers)
They've had the cake decorated.
She's having her hair done.
She's had the wedding dress made.
She's having her nails manicured.
They've had the invitations printed.
They're having the photographs taken.
They had the champagne delivered.
She's having the bouquets delivered.
He had his hair cut.
He's having his feet massaged.
He had his suit fitted.
They'll be having the photographs developed.
He had his shirt pressed.
She'll be having her wedding dress dry-cleaned.

6 Transport
Exercise 1
1 = Car; 2 = Bus; 3 = Train; 4 = Plane; 5 = Bicycle; 6 = Ferry

	1	2	3	4	5	6
get into/ out of	✔					
get on/ off		✔	✔	✔	✔	✔
take off/ land				✔		
ride					✔	
drive	✔	✔	✔			
catch/miss	✔	✔	✔			✔
board				✔		✔
overtake	✔	✔			✔	
park	✔	✔				

Exercise 2
car: traffic lights one-way street
joyrider tyres trailer slip-road
spare tyre service station lay-by
seat-belt horn tunnel
traffic jam
bus: traffic lights tunnel tyres
timetable spare tyre lay-by
horn traffic jam season ticket
ticket collector
train: carriage tunnel ticket
collector platform timetable
track porter coach
season ticket
plane: runway check-in desk
trolley tyres seat-belt cargo
hand luggage Customs cabin
life jacket
bicycle: handlebars tyres crash
helmet traffic lights
one-way street
ferry: deck life jacket gangway
jetty port horn cargo cabin
Customs

Exercise 3
a OVERTAKE
b CARAVAN
c RUNWAY
d GANGWAY
e SLIP ROAD
f PORTER
g CARGO
h SERVICE STATION
i TUNNEL
j HANDLEBARS
k ROUND TRIP
l TRAFFIC JAM
m CUSTOMS
n CHECK-IN DESK
Mystery word: TRANSPORTATION

7 Prepositions of movement
a above/over/behind
b out of
c along/down/up
d out of/through
e along/down/up
f over
g to
h on/onto
i round
j along/up/down
k past
l into
m beside/by/at
n in
o off
p over
q across
r towards
s to
t through
u on
v by/beside
w against
x past/by
y over

8 Word stress
Exercise 1
a explorer exploration
b Japan Japanese
c optimist optimistic
d industry industrial
e economy economics
f politics politician
g origins original
h opera operatic

Exercises 2 and 3
●● opera chocolates business broadcast
●● Japan create abroad hotel unique
●●● explorer religion delicious destruction illegal develop

●●● optimist industry politics origins traveller backpacker privileged organize passenger caravan photograph
●●● Japanese overtake
●●●● exploration optimistic economics politician operatic prehistoric
●●●● industrial economy original discovery inhabitant experiment photographer

Unit 3
1 Past Simple and Past Perfect
Exercise 1
a fell
b had fallen
c had felt/felt
d felt
e had had
f had
g tore
h had torn
i had cost
j cost
k flew
l had never flown
m caught
n had caught
o had been
p were

Exercise 2
✓: feel have cost catch
✗: fall tear fly be

2 Past Simple or Continuous?
a played/was playing were winning lost
b was coughing/coughed didn't get
c was playing hit made
d wasn't thinking had
e picked gave made
f was pruning heard appeared stung
g was snowing got up were making put raced

3 Past Simple or Past Perfect?
a didn't find had given
b rang had just returned
c had wanted did had come
d had/had had burst/had burst broke/had broken left/had left
e went had been had had decided
f had been/was became had earned gave
g had eaten didn't fit
h came had done had made

4 Time expressions
Exercise 1
a 3 b 4 c 2 d 5 e 1 f 9 g 6
h 10 i 8 j 7 k 13 l 14 m 15
n 12 o 11

Exercise 2
a Two years ago, while I was working in Paris, my grandfather died.
b As soon as I had fed the cat I did my homework.
c First I had a shower, then I got dressed.
d Since I was a child I had always wanted to go to Australia, and I finally went last year.
e As he posted the letter he realized he hadn't put a stamp on it.
f By the time he'd finished speaking, most of the audience had fallen asleep.

g Once I'd told him the truth I felt better.

h Until I tried/had tried waterskiing I hadn't believed/didn't believe how difficult it would be.

5 Puss in Boots

Exercise 1

1 had been staying, had just waved
2 were driving, was miaowing
3 crashed into
4 caught fire, arrived, pulled them out
5 had raced back
6 leapt up, ran away, was carrying
7 hadn't found
8 was lying awake, heard, woke, had been dreaming
9 crept, the noise was coming from, were bleeding, had found his way, had been walking
10 knitted, wore

Exercise 2

a were driving
b had been staying
c had just waved
d was miaowing
e crashed into
f caught fire
g arrived
h pulled them out
i had raced back
j was carrying
k leapt up
l ran away
m hadn't found
n was lying awake
o had been dreaming
p heard
q woke
r crept
s the noise was coming from
t had been walking
u had found his way
v were bleeding
w knitted
x wore

Exercise 3

a Who had Jim and Rita been staying with?
b Why was Whiskers miaowing?
c What happened to their car?
d What was Rita doing when the car exploded?
e Why did Whiskers run away?/Why did Whiskers leap into the air?
f What had Rita been dreaming about?
g How long had Whiskers been walking (for)?
h Why did Rita knit him some baby bootees?

6 Active to passive

a A medieval temple was discovered underneath the new housing estate.
b The races were held indoors because it was raining.
c Our house had been broken into and all my jewellery had been stolen.
d The leisure centre had been booked for a children's party on Saturday.
e The dishwasher was being fixed so I couldn't leave the house.
f Our hotel room still hadn't been cleaned when we returned.
g The fish hadn't been cooked for long enough. It was still raw!
h New traffic lights were being put up at the crossroads.

7 Active and passive

Maudie Walker

a had just succeeded
b was smiling
c waving
d was overcome
e suffered
f died

Major Summerfield

a had died
b was fighting
c was struck
d fell
e wasn't badly injured
f was fishing
g had just caught
h struck
i were paralysed
j was being buried
k shattered

Rueben Tice

a wasn't
b was working
c hadn't slept
d was putting/had been putting
e exploded
f was hit
g was killed
h was covered

8 The world of literature

Poetry: nursery rhyme   character   ballad   verse   paperback   hardback

Prose: plot   chapter   autobiography   character   best-seller   review   science fiction   novelist   critic   blockbuster   fairy tale   hardback   whodunnit   paperback   thriller

Drama: plot   act   director   character   backstage   leading role   science fiction   script   review   blockbuster   props   scenery   critic   rehearsal   playwright   whodunnit   stalls   thriller   standing ovation   performance

9 Words commonly confused

1 a 're waiting for
  b is expected
  c are looking forward to
2 a ground
  b floor
  c ground
3 a Actually
  b at the moment
  c really
4 a alone   lonely
  b lone
5 a nervous
  b embarrassed
  c ashamed
6 a was usually taken
  b brought/brings
  c fetch
7 a Have you seen
  b were watching
  c Look at

10 Phrasal verbs type 1

Exercise 1

show off – boast
find out – discover
doze off – fall asleep
hold on – wait
speak up – talk louder
set off – begin a journey
blow up – explode
settle down – have a calmer, more stable life
turn up – arrive
own up – admit responsibility
cheer up – be happier
go out – stop burning
shut up – be quiet
stay in – not go out, stay at home

Exercise 2

a owns up
b went out
c 'll turn up
d set off
e Cheer up
f showing off
g stay in
h settled down
i dozed off
j find out
k Shut up
l Hold on
m Speak up
n blew up

11 Diphthongs

Exercise 1

a /peɪ/
b /raɪt/
c /fəʊn/
d /raʊnd/
e /dɪə/
f /bɔɪ/
g /tʊə/
h /feə/

Exercise 2

a near
b care
c throw
d flight
e page
f join
g town
h fewer

Exercise 3

/iː/ (2)   /eɪ/ (1)
/uː/ (4)   /əʊ/ (3)
/ɔː/ (5)   /ʌ/ (6)
/ɜː/ (8)   /ɪə/ (7)
/ɜː/ (10)   /ɔː/ (9)
/aʊ/ (11)   /əʊ/ (12)
/uː/ (13)   /əʊ/ (14)
/uːz/ (17)   /əʊz/ (15)   /əʊs/ (16)
/uːz/ (19)   /uːs/ (18)
/ɒm/ (22)   /uːm/ (21)   /əʊm/ (20)
/ɒl/ (23)   /əʊl/ (24)   /ʌm/ (26)
 /əʊm/ (25)
/eɪ/ (27)   (28)
/eɪ/ (29)   /e/ (30)
/ʊ/ (33)   /uː/(32)   /ʌ/ (31)
/ʊd/ (35)   /əʊld/ (34)
/əʊ/ (38)   /ʌ/ (36)   /ɒ/ (37)

Unit 4

1 Countable or uncountable?

a luggage
b food
c cash
d corn
e fruit
f unemployment
g accommodation
h health
i music
j traffic

2 some or any?

a any
b some/any   any
c Some   any
d some   any
e any   any
f some   some

3 much or many?

a Is there much work …?
b I didn't spend much time …
c Did they do much research …?
d They couldn't give me much information …
e There is too much traffic …
f I didn't have too many problems …

4 The canteen

Exercise 1 (Sample answers)

a There are lots of cheese sandwiches.
b There are a few ham sandwiches.
c There's a huge amount of spaghetti.
d There's only a little rice and vegetable curry.
e There are a few hamburgers.
f There are no chips.
g There's hardly any fruit salad.
h There are a couple of bananas.
i There aren't many doughnuts.
j There's hardly any apple juice.

Exercise 2

a 's lots
b a few
c 's only a little
d aren't any (left)
e a little
f are a few
g 's only a little
h 've got a couple
i a little
j lots

5 very little, a little, very few, a few, fewer, less

a a few chips
b a little whisky
c Children have less respect for their teachers than they used to.
d very few
e a little Swedish
f Fewer people
g Very few people
h a few years
i There's very little I can do …
j a few of them

6 From riches to rags

Exercise 1

a many
b hardly any/very little
c a few
d a huge amount
e no
f few
g nobody
h much
i most
j several
k all
l a large number
m very little/hardly any
n fewer
o less
p none
q a lot
r a couple
s anything
t Something

Exercise 2

a Fred has no relatives.
b Fred didn't talk to anyone about his grief.
c People were friendly to Fred because he had a lot of money.
d He invested a lot/a huge amount of his money.
e Fred had a little money left when Barings went bankrupt.
f Nobody helped Fred when he ran out of money.
g Fred has made a couple of real friends.
h Fred has learned a lot from his experience.

7 something, anybody, everyone, nowhere …

Exercise 1

a somewhere
b anyone
c everywhere anywhere
d anything
e everything
f nothing
g nobody/no one
h anywhere
i someone
j something anything
k anyone
l Everyone/Everybody

Exercise 2

a He told the police that he knew nothing.
  He didn't tell the police anything.
b I think they live somewhere in London.
  I don't mind. I'll live anywhere in London.

c Anybody can cook. It's easy.
Nobody phoned you. Sorry.
d I've searched everywhere.
I can't find it anywhere.
e I thought I'd know somebody at the party.
I didn't know anyone at the party.
f My parents never took me anywhere when I was a kid.
My parents took me everywhere when I was young.
g Jane always got everything she wanted.
Jane didn't have anything to wear.
h I've already had something to eat.
I've had nothing to eat.

8 all or every?

a everything   b Everything   c All
d Every   e All   f All   g All
h all the   i everything   j all
k Every

9 A piece of cake!

Exercise 1

a jar of honey   a can of beer/soup/
Coke   a slice of bread/cake
a tube of toothpaste   a piece of cake/
paper/bread   a loaf of bread
a bottle of beer/Coke   a bar of
soap/chocolate   a box of chocolates
a tin of soup   a sheet of paper

Exercise 2

a a piece/slice
of cake
b a tin/can of
soup
c sheets of paper
d a box of
chocolates
e bar of chocolate

f slice of bread
g many cans/
bottles of beer
h bar of soap
i a jar of special
apple blossom
honey

10 Prepositions and nouns

Exercise 1

A
above/below/on average   **on** foot
under arrest   **over/under** £500
above/below/over/under 75%
above/below freezing
over/under 18 years old
under new management
on holiday   **under** pressure
on business

B
at/by midnight   **during/in** the night
by/on New Year's Day
by/during/in the winter
by/on Friday afternoon
at/by/during the weekend
in/on time   **in** a fortnight's time
during/in the rush hour   **in** his forties

Exercise 2

a over   b in   c on   d at   e on
f on   g By   h On   i at   j during/
in   k below   l under   m in   n by
o in

11 Sentence stress

a Well, I know he earns a lot more
than me.

b What do you mean? He's already
bought a brand new one.

c Didn't you know that all of Frank's
clothes are designer labels?

d He has loads of them.

e No, in fact he's in Florida on
holiday.

f Really? The girl I saw him with had
short, brown hair.

12 Phonetics

Exercises 1 and 2

Fruit: 'grapefruit   pear   'pineapple
'cherry   'melon   'orange   plum
'strawberry   'raspberry   avo'cado
'mango

Vegetables: 'carrot   'cauliflower
pea   po'tato   'cabbage   leek
cour'gette   'parsnip   'cucumber
'sweetcorn   'spinach   'onion

Unit 5

1 Question tags

a You're going to work harder from
now on, aren't you?

b I'll see you next week, won't I?

c Kate's leaving soon, isn't she?

d You'll ring when you get there,
won't you?

e Our plane takes off at 4 p.m.,
doesn't it?

f The decorators will have finished by
next week, won't they?

g You aren't getting married next
week, are you?

h We won't need tickets to get in, will
we?

i We'll be millionaires one day, won't
we?

j Max won't be coming, will he?

2 will or going to?

a A 'm going to   B 'll
b A are going to   B 'll
c A 'm going to   'll   B 'll
d A 's going to/will   B 'll
e A 'm not going to   B 'll
f A 'll   B 'm going to   'll
g A 'm going to   B 'll   'll
h A 're going to/'ll   B 'll

3 What does John say?

a I'll buy her a present.

b I'm going to study hard …

c I'm seeing/going to see …

d I think Manchester United will/are
going to win on Saturday.

e I'm sorry. I'm going to be late.

f My sister is going to have/having a
baby next March.

g My plane takes off at 7.30 a.m.
from London, Heathrow.

h I'll be lying on a beach in Spain this
time next week.

4 Future Cont. or Perfect?

a I'll have become …
b I'll be running my own …
c I'll have moved to California.
d I'll be living in a mansion …
e I'll have joined a …
f I'll have married a …

g I'll be earning over …
h I'll have given up smoking.

5 A Hollywood interview

Exercise 1

a are getting
b will have
exchanged
c 'll make
d are going to
tell
e are having
f will you be
inviting
g are coming

h will arrive
i are coming
j won't be
coming
k are going to
have
l doesn't start
m will be arriving
n leaves
o 'll be

Exercise 2

a will be
expecting
b 'll own
c will have fallen
out
d will be having/
will have had

e will be working
f will be worried/
worrying
g won't have
remembered/
won't remember
h will want
i won't agree

6 Correcting mistakes

a A What <u>are you doing</u> this
weekend?
B ✔

b A ✔
B Oh, no! What <u>am I going to do</u>?

c A Is it true that Rachel <u>is getting
married</u> to …
B ✔

d A ✔
B Yuk! You<u>'ll have to wake me up</u>.
I can never get up …

e A ✔
B … You<u>'ll be getting</u> …

f A ✔
B … It<u>'ll only take</u> a …

g A ✔
B … We<u>'re going to stay/
're staying</u> at home.

h A I'll ring you as soon as I <u>arrive</u>.
B ✔

7 Future time clauses

a won't get   eat sensibly.
b 're not moving to   find/have found
c 'll love/'re going to love   meet
d Are you going to learn   're
e won't go to bed   have
f 's going to be   've finished
g don't do   will you have to
h will deal   are
i 'll feel   have/have had
j try/have tried   'll never use

8 Health

Exercise 1 (Sample answers)

a The nurse took the patient's
temperature.

b The surgeon performed a difficult
operation.

c The accident victim was carried on
a stretcher.

d The toddler fell over and grazed his
knee.

e The teenager had spots on her face.

f The pregnant woman felt faint in
the smoky atmosphere.

g The old man had a heart attack.

h The tennis player sprained her
wrist.

i The racing driver was lucky to
survive the crash.

j The soldier was wounded in the
attack.

k The gardener was stung by a wasp.

l The ferry passengers felt sea-sick
during the crossing.

m The holidaymaker suffered from
sunburn.

Exercise 2

a injured
b dislocated
c stitches
d pain
e a rash

f allergic to
g a blister
h dizzy
i run down
j damages

9 Hot Verbs be and have

Exercise 1

be on the safe side   in touch with sb
no point in doing sth   off colour
out of one's mind   up to date
in charge of sb/sth   on one's mind
have the nerve to do sth   sb round
a word with sb   a ball
no chance of doing sth

Exercise 2

a be a bit off
colour
b 'll be in touch
c 're having Mel
and Andy
round
d 's always on
my mind
e 've been out
of my mind
f have a word
with you

g had the nerve
h to be on the
safe side
i have no chance
of
j 'm in charge of
k having a ball
l 's no point in
m be up to date

10 Phrasal verbs types 2 and 3

a talked it over
b take after her
c sort it out
d gone off her
e call it off
f put them away

g look after him
h look into it
i get over it
j work it out
k putting me
down

11 Sounds and spelling

Exercise 1

a won't   /əʊ/   want   /ɒ/
b walk   /ɔː/   work   /ɜː/
c wonder   /ʌ/   wander   /ɒ/
d woman   /ʊ/   women   /ɪ/
e warm   /ɔː/   worm   /ɜː/
f word   /ɜː/   ward   /ɔː/
g wear   /eə/   weary   /ɪə/
h weight   /eɪ/   weird   /ɪə/

Exercise 2

a phone
b blood
c love
d through

e weak
f lower
g north

h height
i pear
j layer

Unit 6

1 General knowledge quiz

1 b   2 a   3 a   4 c   5 b   6 a
7 c   8 b   9 c   10 a

2 Defining or non-defining?

Exercise 1

a D b D c ND d D e ND
f D g ND h D i ND j ND

Exercise 2

a … who could teach me …
b … that has four bedrooms.
c … *Romeo and Juliet*, which is one of the best films I've ever seen.
d … that sells second-hand furniture?
e Marilyn Monroe, whose real name was Norma Jean Baker, died of an overdose of barbiturates.
f … who lose their temper …
g My computer, which I bought just last year, is already out of date.
h I met a girl I went to school with.
i Professor James Williams, who is considered to be the world's expert on butterflies, will …
j I bought a ham and pickle sandwich, which I ate immediately.

3 Punctuation and omitting the pronoun

a The thing ~~that~~ I most regret is not going to university.
b My two daughters, who are 16 and 13, are both interested in dancing.
c (no change)
d (no change)
e (no change)
f Salt, whose qualities have been known since prehistoric times, is used to season and preserve food.
g The CD ~~that~~ I bought yesterday doesn't work.
h You know the book ~~that~~ you paid £20 for? I just got it for £5.
i (no change)
j Devon, where my mother's family comes from, is famous …

4 All relative pronouns

Exercise 1

a Have I told you recently how much I love you?
b I have to do what I believe to be right.
c I love garlic in all my food, which is why I'm always brushing my teeth.
d We're emigrating to Australia, where my brother lives.
e I met a girl whose hair came down to her waist.
f I passed all my exams, which greatly surprised my teachers.
g Let me know when you expect to arrive.
h Being generous, I'll buy you whatever you want.

Exercise 2

a who
b that
c where
d which
e (nothing)
f whose
g which
h (nothing)
i where
j that
k whose
l (nothing)
m where
n which
o Whatever

5 Prepositions in relative clauses

a This is the book I was telling you about.
b She's a friend I can always rely on.
c That's the man the police were looking for.
d She recommended a book by Robert Palmer, who I'd never heard of.
e The carpet which you paid £500 for has been reduced to £200.
f The Prime Minister, whose views I agree with, gave a good speech.
g He spoke about the environment, which I care deeply about.
h What's that music you're listening to?
i Her mother, who she looked after for many years, died last week.
j My daughter has started smoking, which I disapprove of.

6 Participles as adjectives

a screaming
b satisfied
c disgusting
d confusing
e loaded
f exposed
g conceited
h frightening
i exhausting
j disappointing
k boring
l tiring
m unexpected
n disturbing
o thrilling
p relaxing
q blocked
r disappointed
s well-behaved
t promising

7 Participle clauses

Exercise 1

a People living …
b Letters posted …
c The train standing …
d … passengers trapped …
e … litter dropped …
f … house overlooking …

Exercise 2

a finishing
b stolen
c saying
d Feeling
e borrowed
f knowing
g explaining
h Taking
i directed
j studying

8 I didn't know what to do

a … what time to invite people.
b … whether to invite Suzie or not.
c … how to use e-mail.
d … what drink to buy.
e … how many people to invite.

9 Micro Mad Max

a 10 b 13 c 7 d 9 e 1 f 2
g 14 h 4 i 11 j 3 k 5 l 6
m 12 n 8

10 a three-mile walk

a a ten-pound note
b a four-week language course
c a three-hour drive
d a three-course meal
e a two-week holiday
f a two-hour delay
g a ten-page letter
h a three-year course
i a ten-year sentence
j a five-star hotel
k a 30-mile-an-hour speed limit
l a two-hundred-year-old house

11 People, places, and things

People: obstinate cunning spoilt aggressive arrogant easy-going
Places: breathtaking unspoilt picturesque deserted overgrown overcrowded
Things: automatic hand-made accurate waterproof artificial long-lasting

12 Similar words

a illegible
b unreadable
c childish
d childlike
e sensitive
f sensible
g truthful
h true
i intolerant
j intolerable
k economic
l economical

13 Adjective + preposition

a of b with, for c for d of
e of f with/in g from, to
h about i to j of k of l for
m for n about o with

14 Silent consonants

Exercise 1

A
industry computer continent recipe eccentric insect lamp hooligan stadium forest citizen

B
bomb listen gadget honest receipt mortgage fasten heirloom whistle straight fascinating sandwich exhausted

Exercise 2

a scientific
b psychologist
c handsome
d research
e Christmas
f friendship
g climb
h grandfather
i campaign
j Wednesday
k calm
l whisky

Unit 7

1 Basic verb patterns

a I enjoy cooking. I find it very creative.
b I look forward to seeing you again soon.
c You need to book if you want to eat at *Guido's*.
d I finished painting the bathroom last night.
e My dad promised to buy me a stereo if I passed my exams.
f I hope to see you again soon.
g Anna chose to wear her black suede skirt for the party.
h What do you feel like doing tonight?
i I can't afford to buy anything. I'm broke.
j I can't stand waiting in queues. It really annoys me.
k Beth helped me do the washing-up.
l What would you like to do tonight?

2 Using a dictionary

Exercise 1

a … they stopped to ask for …
b ✔
c I stopped playing …

d The rain was so heavy … to stop the kitchen from flooding.
e … stopped me to ask why …
f … the sun stopped shining.
g ✔
h … stop his son from going to …

Exercise 2

a ✔
b I avoid travelling …
c Have you considered working …
d We expected him to arrive …
e ✔
f I've arranged to collect …
g ✔
h I can't help loving …
i I offered to give …
j ✔
k ✔
l I suggest we go to a restaurant …
m I want you to come home early.

3 More complex verb patterns

Exercise 1 (Sample answers)

My brother wants me to fix his bike.
Our hosts would hate us to be late.
My aunt would love me to visit her more often.
The doctor warned his patient not to work so hard.
My parents expect me to do well in my exams.
The guide advised the tourists to stay close.
The policeman told the driver to slow down.
We invited all our friends to come to a party.
The teacher made her class do the exercise again.
My grandparents let us do what we wanted.
I'd like my son to take over my business.

Exercise 2

a I didn't expect to see Ben …
b We've been invited to dinner …
c I need to have a hair-cut.
d I'm looking forward to seeing you in June.
e I can't decide what to have for dessert.
f The teacher let us go home early.
g But she made us do …
h Do you mind waiting for a minute?
i I'd rather have tea.
j I suggest we wait before we …
k She offered to lend me some money.
l He asked me not to make a noise.
m I apologized to my neighbours for waking them.

4 -ing or infinitive?

a to think / getting
b to lock / falling
c making / to make
d to buy / meeting
e to do / asking
f to play / to rain
g to speak / painting
h cooking / to cook / to pay

5 Adjectives, nouns, and prepositions

Exercise 1

a impossible   e delighted

b nice
c safe
d ~~mean~~
f kind
g sorry
h interesting

Exercise 2
a time to go
b way to skin
c idea to visit
d anyone to talk
e need to shout
f things to do
g money to pay
h nothing to wear

Exercise 3
a for arriving
b by doing
c about going
d without asking
e with having
f for making
g at remembering
h of buying
i for coming
j like going
k of being stung

6 Forms of the infinitive
a have forgotten
b to be selected
c to pay
d to have met
e to be dry-cleaned
f to be having
g to disturb
h be working
i to have seen
j to be recognized
k have told
l to be handed

7 I don't want to
a 7 b 9 c 6 d 2 e 1 f 10
g 4 h 3 i 5 j 8

8 The house that Jack built
a to work
b to pay
c leaving
d to do
e to lend
f listening
g working
h to make
i repaying
j to give
k to celebrate
l doing
m to build
n living
o being

9 Verbs of perception
a singing
b slam
c cooking
d playing sunbathing
e pick rip
f waiting
g being built
h laughing
i eat
j shoplifting take put

10 Compound nouns
a blood test blood pressure blood donor
b campsite building site bomb-site
c waterfall water-melon water-skiing
d greenhouse greengrocer green salad
e nightclub nightmare night shift
f briefcase suitcase bookcase
g paper bag plastic bag shoulder-bag
h rainbow raincoat raindrop
i sunshine sunrise sunset
j roadworks road sign road rage
k blackboard floorboard notice-board
l daylight daybreak day-dream
m handshake handwriting handbook
n ice-cube iceberg ice-rink
o birthday cake birthday present birthday card
p landscape landlady landslide
q sports car sports centre sports ground
r address book visitors' book notebook

11 Phrasal verbs type 4
a away from
b down on
c on with
d up to
e down on
f away with
g up for
h away with
i up with
j out with
k up against
l in with

12 Weak and strong forms
Exercise 1
a She isn't going to learn from this experience, but he is.
b I've heard that you're thinking of moving from London. Are you?
c They have dinner at seven, don't they?
d You'll be able to get a ticket for me, won't you?
e I've got no idea who this letter's from.
f Can't you remember who Bill used to work for?
g I've been waiting for you to come. Where were you?
h We'd been looking forward to coming for ages, then at the last minute we weren't able to.
i Won't you sit down for a couple of minutes?

Exercise 2
A What are you doing at the weekend?
A We're going to Scotland. Do you want to come too?
A We've decided to camp. None of us can afford to pay for a hotel.
A No we won't. We've got strong tents, lots of warm clothes, and thick sleeping bags.
A Of course we have, and it's pretty warm for October.
A Excellent. I'll tell the others. They'll be delighted. We'll pick you up at six on Friday. See you then. Goodbye.

Unit 8

1 How certain?
a ✔✔ b ✔ c ✔✔ d ✔✔ e ✔
f ✔✔ g ✔ h ✔✔ i ✔ j ✔✔
k ✔✔ l ✔✔

2 Present probability
a She must be missing her boyfriend.
b It'll be Tom.
c She can't still be sleeping.
d They should be in the top drawer.
e They could be having a party.
f He must have a deadline to meet.
g It might be difficult driving to work.
h She may be hiding in the wardrobe.

3 Past probability
Exercise 1
a She must have got engaged to Andy.
b He can't have cut it for ages.
c They must have been doing something naughty.
d She must have been making a cake.
e They can't/must/might have gone without me.

f He can't have had a party last night.
g They should have arrived home by now.
h She might have mislaid my number.

Exercise 2
a It must have been blown down by the wind.
b They must have been washed with something red.
c It can't have been mended properly.
d It can't have been given enough to eat.
e They can't have been watered for a long time.
f It must have been shattered by a stone.

Exercise 3 (Sample answers)
If I go to India I can see the Taj Mahal.
If I go to India I will see …
If I go to India I might see …
If I go to India I may see …
If I went to India I would see …
If I went to India I might see …
If I went to India I could see …
If I'd gone … I might have seen …
If I'd gone … I would have seen …
If I'd gone … I could have seen …

4 Deductions about the present and past
a must be making
b could have used might have climbed up
c would have been
d may have been joking can't have spent must have misheard
e should be touching down must be will already have landed.
f could be snowing can snow

5 Meaning check
a ability
b permission
c permission
d advice
e asking
f manage
g sure
h possibility
i gave …
not necessary
j ought

6 Which modals fit?
Exercise 1
a should/ought to
b Can/Could/May/Might
c must/have to/should
d can
e will/could/may/might/should/ought to
f can
g have to
h could/may/might/should/ought to/must
i can/could/may/should/ought to/must/have to
j must/have to

Exercise 2
a shouldn't
b don't have to
c couldn't
d won't
e cannot
f was able to
g should have gone
h mustn't

7 Obligation and permission
Exercise 1
1 will not marry
5 may not visit

2 can only keep
3 should command
4 must be at home
6 cannot ride
7 shall sweep
8 will dress must be
9 may not travel

Exercise 2
a had to couldn't
b had to weren't allowed to/couldn't
c didn't have to was also allowed couldn't/weren't allowed to
d weren't allowed to/couldn't
e were forbidden to/weren't allowed to/couldn't
f had to weren't allowed to/couldn't

8 Present to past
a I had to take …
b They must have been away …
c We couldn't see the top …
d He can't/couldn't have been …
e We weren't allowed to/were forbidden to/couldn't …
f He wouldn't go to bed.
g That would have been John …
h You should have been more careful.
i You didn't have to do this exercise.

9 Positive to negative
a You mustn't stop here.
b We didn't have to learn …
c They didn't have to take …
d He can't be speaking Swedish.
e We didn't have to wear …
f You won't have to help me …

10 need and needn't have
Exercise 1
a V b M c V d V e V f M
g M h V i V j M

Exercise 2
a mustn't
b needn't/ don't have to
c have to/need to
d don't need to/ don't have to
e needn't have woken
f didn't need to take/didn't have to take
g got to
h needn't have bought

11 Words that go together
a C b A c D d B e D f C
g B h A i C j A k B l D
m C n D

12 A word puzzle
1 OSCAR
2 PREMIÈRE
3 GLAMOROUS
4 JETSETTER
5 FANCLUB
6 AUTOGRAPH
7 SOCIALITE
8 PENTHOUSE
9 LIMOUSINE
10 MODEL
11 ARISTOCRAT
Mystery word: CELEBRITIES

13 Verb + preposition
a for b about/for/at c of d from
e in f to g in h in i to/with
j to, about

14 Consonant clusters and connected speech

Exercise 1

a doesn't
b shouldn't
c mustn't
d muscles
e crashed
f distinctly
g special
h grumbled
i thrilled
j marvellous
k excitement
l sixth
m impressed
n length
o comfortable

Exercise 2

a The car windscreen's smashed.
b My uncle's sprained his ankle.
c This cream doesn't taste fresh.
d You don't have to scream.
e These white jeans must have shrunk.
f She arrived dressed in the latest fashion.
g He doesn't know his own strength.
h He can't have fixed it properly.

Unit 9

1 Negative auxiliaries

a don't
b didn't
c haven't
d aren't
e isn't
f won't/ isn't
g 'm not
h doesn't
i hadn't
j hasn't

2 no, not, -n't, or none?

a not b n't c not d not e no
f Not g none h no i n't j not
k Not l none m No n no
o None p Not

3 Making sentences mean the opposite (Sample answers)

a None of the students passed the exam, so their teacher was furious/disappointed.
b Tom was an unsuccessful businessman who achieved very little in his life.
c Our house is easy to find. No one ever gets lost.
d We had a terrible time in Venice. There were too many people there.
e You mustn't exercise your ankle. Try not to move it at all.
f I don't have to iron my shirt. I'm not going out tonight.
g You don't need to/needn't come with me. I'll go on my own.
h I wasn't in a hurry because I didn't need to go to the shops.
i You ought not to have given the dog anything to eat.
j I told you not to go to work. Why aren't you in bed?

4 I don't think you're right

a I don't suppose you've got …
b The machine doesn't seem to be working.
c I didn't think it was going to rain.
d They don't want their daughter to marry a footballer.
e I didn't expect to see you …
f I don't suppose you've seen …
g I don't think I'd like snails.
h I don't expect you remember me.

i She doesn't seem to like her job.
j I don't believe she got grade A …

5 Buzz Aldrin

a When did man first walk on the moon?
b Who went first?
c How long has Buzz Aldrin been travelling the world?
d Where was he born?
e Which military academy did he graduate from?
f Where did he serve as a pilot?
g When was he chosen as an astronaut?
h When was Apollo 11 launched to the moon?
i How long did the mission last?
j What happened to Buzz when he returned?
k What did he suffer from?
l How many children did he have from his first marriage?
m How many times has he been married?
n Who saved him from self-destruction?
o Who do they live with?
p How many cars do they have?
q What sort of books has he written?
r When was Encounter with Tiber published?
s What does he do with himself these days?

6 Dialogues

a Who made that mess …? What were you doing? When are you going to tidy it up?
b What was it like? Who did you talk to? What about? What went wrong? What about?
c What for/Why? Who was he attacked by/Who by? What was he doing/Where was he when …? How is he? Which hospital was he taken to? How long is he going to be in hospital?

7 Questions and prepositions

Exercise 1

a by b to c at d on e for
f in g about h of i from
j with

Exercise 2

a What about?
b Where to?
c What about?
d How long for?
e Who for?
f Who to?
g What with?

8 How …? and What … like?

a What's he like?
b How was school today?
c What was the food like?
d How was your journey?
e What's the weather like?
f How is/was she?
g What's it like?
h How's your job these days?

9 Negative questions

a 2 b 1 c 3 d 4 e 5 f 6
g 8 h 7 i 9 j 10 k 12 l 11

10 Antonyms and synonyms

A	B
unkind	*cruel*
dishonest	deceitful
incredible	unbelievable
disappear	vanish
unfair	biased
displeased	annoyed
discontinue	halt
unfasten	undo
abnormal	exceptional
unemployed	redundant
unfriendly	hostile
distrust	suspect
unprofessional	amateur
unknown	anonymous
discover/uncover	reveal
unsafe	hazardous
abuse/misuse	damage
improbable	unlikely
unimportant	trivial
unemotional	reserved

11 Hot Verbs keep and lose

Exercise 1

keep calm a promise going in touch with sb sb company your nerve a secret sb waiting your temper fit
lose weight your way your nerve your temper

Exercise 2

a keep in touch
b lost my temper
c keep going
d keep a secret
e lost my nerve
f keep fit
g Keep calm
h lost my way

12 Phrasal verbs and nouns that go together

Exercise 1

come up with a new idea, a plan
beat up an old man, a victim of a crime
break into a house, a flat, to steal something
break off a relationship, an engagement
bring out a new product on the market
bring up children to be honest and hard-working
clear out a cupboard and throw out what you don't want
count on your best friend to help you
deal with a problem, a complaint, a difficult customer
drop out of a university course after one year
fit in with the other people in the group
look up to someone you respect
point out a fact that someone might not be aware of
take back what I said – I didn't mean it
tell off a naughty child

Exercise 2

a clear out
b are bringing out
c broke into
d beat him up
e looked up to
f I take it all back.
g I'll point him out
h come up with
i told Tom off
j deal with
k fit in with
l drop out of
m count on
n brought me up

13 Intonation in question tags

Exercise 1

a aren't you? ▼
b wasn't it? ▼
c could you? ▲
d isn't he? ▼
e isn't it? ▼
f has he? ▲
g aren't I? ▼
h have you? ▲
i isn't it? ▼
j weren't we? ▼
k would you? ▲
l had we? ▼

Exercise 2

a You like that car, don't you? ▼
b Vanessa, you're going to Rome next week, aren't you? ▲
c That was awful, wasn't it? ▼
d You haven't borrowed my new coat again, have you? ▲
e You couldn't water my plants while I'm away, could you? ▲

Unit 10

1 Tina's diary

Exercises 1 and 2

a usually
b occasionally
c used to (✔)
d frequently
e rarely/ hardly ever
f rarely/ hardly ever
g always
h sometimes
i will
j would (✔)

2 Present habit

Exercise 1

1 d 2 g 3 f 4 e 5 h 6 c 7 b
8 i 9 j 10 a

Exercise 2 (Sample answers)

a She has three a day.
b He's always telling people how clever he is.
c She won't eat anything at all unusual.
d He doesn't play anything.
e They're always buying things.
f He's always sitting at his computer, surfing the Internet.
g She's always watching TV.
h He always expects the worst to happen.
i They *will* eat with their mouths open.
j He never lets you down.

3 used to and would

Exercise 1

a used to
b Did you use to
c never used to/ didn't use to
d Did you use to
e used to
f didn't use to
g did you use to
h Didn't you use to

Exercise 2

1 a, b 2 a 3 a, b, c 4 a, b, c
5 a 6 a, b, c 7 a, b 8 a
9 a, b, c

4 Criticizing other people

Exercise 1

b ✔ d ✔ e ✔ h ✔ i ✔

Exercise 2
My family
a My dad *will* mend/is always mending …
b My brother *will* leave/is always leaving …
c My sister *will* borrow/is always borrowing …
d Uncle Tom *will* smoke/is always smoking …
e My grandpa *would* chew/was always chewing …
f Our great-grandma *wouldn't* turn on/was always turning off …

5 Henry's £4.5 million secret
Exercise 1
a l   b 2   c l   d 3   e 2   f l   g 2
h l   i 3   j l   k 2   l l   m 3   n 2
o 3   p 3

Exercise 2
a believe   d didn't   g always
b to   e use   h inherited
c would   f used

6 *get, become, or be*?
a get upset
b became ill
c 'm getting better
d to become a pilot
e 'll be ready   'm just getting dressed   've been ready
f 're lost
g are getting/ are going to get/ have got divorced
h became clear
i got to know   got to like
j aren't used to
k has become a bit of a bore
l 'm tired
m gets dark
n is becoming more widespread

7 Money
Exercise 1
A + B
I took out a loan.
I exchanged some traveller's cheques.
I inherited my grandfather's farm.
We don't accept credit cards.
I need change for a fiver.
I earned over £2,000 in interest.

B + C
This new coat was a bargain.
His cheque bounced.
Inflation went up by 2%.
The exchange rate is good at the moment.
My credit card expires at the end of July.
My piggy bank is full of 5p pieces.

Exercise 2
A lesson in thrift at the supermarket
a check-out   i wallet
b bar codes   j cash
c added   k customers
d bill   l cut
e pay   m came to
f salary   n saving
g cheque   o change
h overdrawn   p receipt

8 Verb + object + preposition
a **remind** me so much **of**
b **invest** all our money **in**
c **insured** our car **against**
d **congratulated** me **on**

e **was compensated** … **for**
f **models** herself **on**
g **hide** the truth **from**
h **held** her tightly **against/to**
i **invited** 300 guests **to**
j **brainwashes** people **into**
k **inherit** a penny **from**
l **shouted** abuse **at**
m **forgive** him **for**
n **was accused** … **of**

9 Rhymes and limericks
Exercise 1
should	good	food	nude
bread	said	leaf	chief
choose	lose	taught	court
toes	knows	chef	deaf
hate	weight	through	knew
tight	height	wore	pour
full	wool	brain	reign
pool	fool	leave	grieve
blood	mud	foot	put

Exercise 2
The Pelican
A rare old bird is a pelican
His beak can hold more than his belly can.
   He can take in his beak
   Enough food for a week,
And I'm damned if I know how the hell he can!

The lady from Twickenham
There was a young lady from Twickenham
Whose shoes were too tight to walk quick in 'em.
   She came back from a walk
   Looking whiter than chalk
And she took them both off and was sick in 'em!

Unit 11

1 Real or hypothetical past?
Exercise 1
a ✔   d ✔   h ✔
Sentences b, c, e, f, and g all express hypotheses.

Exercise 2
a ✗   b ✔   c ✗   d ✗   e ✔   f ✗
g ✗   h ✔

Exercise 3
a don't.   d is.   g was.
b didn't. e won't. h don't.
c can't.   f do.

2 Present and past wishes
Exercise 1
I wish you were rich.
I wish I were rich.
I wish you could come.
I wish I could come.
I wish you would come.
I wish you had come.

Exercise 2
a could/ was able to
b wasn't
c didn't
d hadn't gone
e had stayed
f didn't speak/ wouldn't speak
g hadn't spent
h lived

3 Expressions of regret
Exercise 1
a I wish I'd invited him to the party.
b You should have been watching.
c If only I hadn't said that to her.
d I wish I hadn't hit him.
e I'd rather you didn't tell her.
f I wish Megan didn't/wouldn't stay out so late.
g If only we could come …
h I should have worked harder …

Exercise 2 (Sample answers)
a I wish I had a Rolls Royce.
b If only I could get a job.
c If only I could get to sleep. I wish it were morning.
d We should have booked some rooms.
e I wish I'd bought some petrol.
f I wish she'd stop playing. (the cat speaking!)

4 Making excuses
Exercise 1
a If I hadn't had the shellfish, I wouldn't have been ill.
b I would have phoned you if I'd had the time.
c If I'd known the jumper was so expensive, I wouldn't have bought it.
d I wouldn't have believed it if I hadn't seen it with my own eyes.

Exercise 2
a If I'd known your address, I'd have sent you a postcard.
b If I'd known when your birthday was, I'd have bought you a present.
c If I'd set my alarm clock, I wouldn't be late/have been late.
d If I hadn't been taking my wife to hospital, I wouldn't have broken the speed limit.

5 May's disastrous day
Exercise 1
a … she'd set her alarm clock.
b … she hadn't been late again.
c … she wouldn't have locked herself in the toilet and she wouldn't have forgotten to meet Ben for lunch.
d … he wouldn't have ended their relationship.
e … she wouldn't have lost a contact lens.
f … she hadn't lost a contact lens.
g … she wouldn't have had to wait at the bus stop in the pouring rain/ … she wouldn't have got so wet.
h … she hadn't waited at the bus stop in the pouring rain/ … she hadn't got so wet.
i … she hadn't forgotten to meet him three times.
j … it wouldn't have eaten the budgie.

Exercise 2
M Well, if you hadn't <u>ended our relationship, I wouldn't have forgotten to feed the cat and then it wouldn't have eaten the budgie.</u>
M Well, that was Ms Collins' fault. If she hadn't <u>cancelled my business trip, I wouldn't have been upset and</u> <u>locked myself in the toilet and I wouldn't have forgotten to meet you for lunch.</u>
B Ah! Now I understand everything. If you'd remembered <u>to set your alarm clock, you wouldn't have overslept and you wouldn't have been late for work and Ms Collins wouldn't have cancelled your business trip and you wouldn't have been upset and forgotten our date.</u>

6 Revision of all conditionals
a If I still <u>feel</u> sick, I <u>won't go</u> …
b If you <u>sold</u> them, you'<u>d make</u> …
c If I <u>see</u> her, I'<u>ll tell</u> her …
d If Alice <u>hadn't gone</u> … she <u>wouldn't have met</u> …
e 'If she <u>didn't love</u> him, she <u>wouldn't have married</u> him.'
f If you <u>buy</u> …, you <u>get</u> one free.
g A What <u>would</u> you <u>do</u> if you <u>saw</u> a ghost?
   B I'<u>d run</u> a mile.
h If we <u>had brought</u> …, we <u>would know</u> …
i If you <u>hadn't had</u> …, the house <u>would have burnt</u> down.
j If I <u>were</u> you, I'<u>d apologize</u>.
k If he <u>eats</u> cheese, he <u>gets</u> …
l If you <u>listened</u> …, you <u>would have heard</u> … <u>wouldn't be</u> stuck here.

7 Words other than *if*
Exercise 1
a Supposing   e Were
b in case   f as long as
c unless   g Had
d Providing   h Should

Exercise 2
a I won't come unless they invite me.
b Supposing he left you, what would you do?
c I'll join the tennis club provided that you do/join too.
d We're going to install a smoke alarm in case there is a fire.
e She won't get the job unless she learns to speak French.
f Imagine the lifeguard hadn't been there, what would have happened?
g I won't go out this evening in case Paul rings.
h I'll come at 8.00 as long as that's all right with you.

8 Poor rich Mr Briggs
a wish   b provided   c unless
d would   e should   f only   g if
h case   i even   j would   k been
l be   m hadn't   n would   o hadn't

9 Physical appearance or personality?
Exercise 1
Physical appearance: curly spotty skinny freckled wrinkled bald well-built graceful bespectacled agile chubby smart
Personality: brainy nosy cheeky moody two-faced absent-minded narrow-minded quick-tempered affectionate hard-hearted big-headed smart

Exercise 2

to arm a country against the threat of war
to back out of an agreement/the car out of the garage
to elbow someone out of the way
to eye someone with suspicion
to finger the material gently
to foot the bill for the meal
to hand out the books to the class
to head the ball into the net
to shoulder the responsibility/blame
to thumb through a book quickly
to toe the line in a job or organization

Exercise 3

a	handed	g	were armed
b	elbow	h	toe
c	thumbed	i	fingering
d	eyed	j	have backed
e	was footing	k	shoulder
f	headed		

10 Nouns from phrasal verbs

a	breakdown	g	outlook
b	comeback	h	outbreak
c	hangover	i	breakthrough
d	check-up	j	feedback
e	outcome	k	takeaway
f	by-pass	l	downfall

11 Ways of pronouncing -ea-
Exercises 1 and 2

/e/ **bread**: breath breadth deaf thread death breast leapt lead (n) health heaven jealous meant weapon

/iː/ **meat**: scream breathe cease cheat heal beast leap lead (v) reason

/ɪə/ **fear**: dear tear (n) spear clear beard gear theatre weary

/eə/ **wear**: tear (v) bear pear swear

/eɪ/ **break**: steak great

/ɜː/ **learn**: yearn earth pearl hearse search

Unit 12

1 Adding information before and after a noun
Exercise 1

a There's a woman wearing a hat pushing a pram.
b I can see a boy being chased by a dog.
c A man is sitting on a bench reading a newspaper and eating a sandwich.
d There's a gardener with a cap on his head cutting the grass.
e A family is sitting under a tree having a picnic.
f I can see an ice-cream van with a long queue.
g There are some children in rowing boats on the lake.
h Some men are sitting fishing by the side of the lake.
i There's a boy on a hill flying a kite.
j I can see a boy on a bike riding past the lake.

Exercise 2

a	lawn mower	f	ice-cream van
b	litter bin	g	rowing boat
c	tennis racquet	h	fishing rod
d	goal posts	i	mountain bike
e	wheelbarrow	j	rollerblades

Exercise 3

a I'm going on a two-week adventure holiday driving through the Sahara Desert.
b The judge gave her a five-year prison sentence for kidnapping a millionaire's son.
c She's going to do a three-year course in modern languages at Oxford University.
d Mercedes have brought out a new two-door sports car with a top speed of 150 miles per hour.

2 Articles
Exercise 1

a a b the c the d a
e (nothing), a, the f the
g a, (nothing) h the, (nothing)
i a, The, (nothing), the

Exercise 2

a An b the c a d a
e (nothing) f an g a h the
i the j a/the k The l a m the
n the o (nothing) p the q the
r (nothing) s his t The
u (nothing) v an w (nothing)
x (nothing) y the z A

3 Determiners

a	All none	i	Each
b	either both	j	either both
c	both neither	k	Neither
d	every	l	Either
e	each	m	both either
f	each	n	No
g	no every	o	Each
h	every		

4 Demonstratives

a	These	f	that	k	that
b	This	g	this	l	this
c	That	h	these	m	That
d	those	i	this	n	those
e	that	j	this	o	that

5 Emphatic structures

b The thing I don't understand is where he gets his money from.
c What I like about her is her sense of humour.
d It's the dark winter evenings I don't like.
e What those children need is firm guidance.
f The thing I don't like about Jenny is the way she always has to know best.
g It isn't money I want, it's love.
h What I can't stand about John is the fact that he never buys you a drink.
i The thing you have to remember about Kathy is that she's sincere.
j It's the fact that I'm rich and he isn't that makes him jealous.

6 Emphasis in speaking

a I <u>did</u> do it.

b I <u>did</u> it. Sorry.
c I knew <u>John</u> was coming.
d I knew that <u>ages</u> ago.
e <u>I</u> didn't tell her.
f I <u>didn't</u> tell her.
g I <u>told</u> you.
h I like <u>Annie</u>.
i I <u>do</u> like Annie. I think she's <u>great</u>.
j <u>I</u> like her.

7 Word order

a I was born in the middle of winter in 1981.
b She bought a new car with the money her father had left her in his will.
c He walked with a limp, because he had hurt his leg playing football.
d I usually go shopping at Tesco's because the prices are lower.
e I go shopping early on Saturday morning, before everyone else arrives.
f I'm going to London today to buy a new coat for Jack.
g You should put your money in the bank immediately.
h Last year we went to France on holiday, but unfortunately the weather was awful.
i She tidied up her flat quickly/She quickly tidied up her flat, because her parents were coming to stay.
j I'll never understand why she loves him so passionately.

8 The passive voice

a Many of van Gogh's most famous paintings were completed in Arles in 1888, including *Sunflowers*. Just two years later he shot himself at the age of 37.
One of his pictures. Today his art work is among the highest priced in the world. In 1989 *Irises* was bought for $53.9 million.
b I've been invited to Buckingham Palace to collect an award for a book I wrote a few years ago.
c Penicillin was discovered in 1929. Since then, it has saved many lives.
d Scientists working in America have discovered a drug that prevents the common cold. The drug will now be produced commercially, and it should be available soon.

9 Combining nouns

a the back of the chair
b the cat's milk
c toilet paper
d my parents' advice
e a bottle of wine
f road sign
g wine bottles
h The Prime Minister's duties/The duties of the Prime Minister
i The heel of my shoe
j your hair brush
k the end of the film
l today's news
m Underground station
n my parents' wedding anniversary
o The company's success/The success of the company

p a fortnight's holiday
q The government's economic policy/The economic policy of the government
r the local state school
s The annual rate of inflation
t coffee cups
u cup of coffee

10 Hot verbs *set* and *break*
Exercise 1

set off on a journey a bone in plaster fire to sth your alarm clock a good example a new world record your heart on doing sth

break a bone skiing the sound barrier the law the old world record a promise someone's heart the speed limit

Exercise 2

a Teachers should set a good example to …
b You're breaking the speed limit.
c I'll set the alarm clock for …
d It broke his heart …
e I set fire to the kitchen.
f … is breaking the law.
g … do we need to set off?
h He's broken the old world record …
i She's set a new world record.
j I broke my arm … the doctor set my arm in plaster …
k You should never break a promise.
l … it breaks the sound barrier …
m We've set our hearts on moving …

11 Noun + prepositions

a out of b in c on, by d for
e in f between g for h to
i about/on j with k to l of
m on n to o in

12 Nouns and verbs
Exercise 1

Noun	Verb
advice /ədvaɪs/	to advise /ədvaɪz/
use /juːs/	to use /juːz/
abuse /əbjuːs/	to abuse /əbjuːz/
belief /bɪliːf/	to believe /bɪliːv/
relief /rɪliːf/	to relieve /rɪliːv/
grief /griːf/	to grieve /griːv/
excuse /ɪkskjuːs/	to excuse /ɪkskjuːz/
breath /breθ/	to breathe /briːð/
half /haːf/	to halve /haːv/
house /haʊs/	to house /haʊz/
safe /seɪf/	to save /seɪv/
bath /baːθ/	to bathe /beɪð/

Exercise 2

a	belief	g	half half
b	breath	h	use
c	safe	i	being housed
d	abuse	j	excuse
e	bathing	k	grieve
f	relief	l	advice